Mastering Your Sewing Machine

Mastering Your
Sewing Machine

With Myra Coles

Published by Traplet Publications Limited 1996
Traplet House,
Severn Drive,
Upton-upon-Severn,
Worcestershire. WR8 0JL
United Kingdom.

ISBN 1 900371 07 3

Front Cover
A computer graphic based on an old and a new sewing machine.
Cover Illustration by Steaven Heppener

Technical Drawings reproduced by Lee Wisedale

Book Design by Sue Huxley

TRAPLET
PUBLICATIONS

Printed and bound by Stephens & George Limited,
Merthyr Industrial Estate, Dowlais, Merthyr Tydfil, Mid Glamorgan CF48 2TD

acknowledgments

I would like to thank the management and staff of all the major Sewing Machine Manufacturing Companies for their continued help and support in my ventures over the years.

They are too numerous to mention individually by name but they all know who they are . . .

I would particularly like to thank the following Companies for allowing me to use technical information, diagrams and photographs in this book: Bernina, Brother, Frister Rossmann and Janome.

The following Companies and individuals have been continually supportive and helpful to me and I am truly grateful – they have all contributed in some measure to the presentation of this book: Liberty of London, Vilene, Coats Crafts, Empress Mills, International Sewing Notions, The Kilberry Inn, David Knowles, Susie Harris.

Extra thanks to Maggie Swain for permission to use photographs of her superb work and to Stan McCabe for extra photography.

My thanks to Beatrice-Catherine Clark for tremendous enthusiasm and assistance in compiling these pages . . . to my husband Bryan who is always enthusiastic and extremely supportive in my work . . . and to Sue, Lee and Steaven in particular at Traplet Publications who have done a superb job – and made mine easier!

contents

introduction

THE SEWING MACHINE! A title that means all things to all people! Immediately you either think of a basic, little old fashioned hand machine, a state-of-the-art computer model OR one of the very many thousands of models in between the two!

THE SEWING MACHINE is either a work-horse or a creative tool: it can be a method for earning your living, just brought out for the odd repair or a constant 'friend' where you relax and find peace and enjoyment in all manner of projects: it can be the ultimate hobby tool!

THE SEWING MACHINE can be left out all the time in a sewing room, on the dining table, in the conservatory (and elsewhere!). Many are banished to the back of the wardrobe or the cupboard under the stairs when not in use or because they frighten their owners.

THE SEWING MACHINE should be a carefully selected item of personal choice but all too often they are a mis-matched gift from a caring spouse or family – which is why so many are under used!

YES Under used! The majority of machines are under used for a variety of reasons. Second to the one above, is fear! Fear of things mechanical/computerised/new/complicated/uncontrollable/and many more. The third reason is probably as simple as not understanding how to use the machine . . .

It is a fact that the manufacturers handbook can be confusing – although many are getting better. It does not help that many are in three or more languages and some are bad translations from a foreign language. Even if you understand the hand-book the most common complaints about them is that they do not tell you how to use the stitches. Well with respect, why should they! The hand-book should instruct you how to use the machine NOT how to sew: does a manual with a cooker teach you to be a cordon bleu cook or a manual with a stereo system tell you how to appreciate music? NO! So providing that the hand-book/manual that comes with a machine is clear and concise on how to operate the machine it must be considered to be doing its job and you should look elsewhere for the information on how to sew . . . and that is a completely different subject to tackle.

This book will not tell you how to sew either. It will tell you how to use a machine to achieve the stitches and techniques to enable you to sew your own chosen projects, whether they be dress, toys, embroideries, crafty items, cushions and other items for home-making . . . even mending. For once you can use your machine proficiently you can sew anything and everything that your machine has capabilities to provide.

My very first book was written because I was asked to do a trouble-shooting article on sewing machines for a magazine and my answer was No! I believed that if you do everything correctly you will not have problems – unless they are mechanical breakdowns beyond your control, of course. I have no reason to change that view because the intervening years have proved me right time and time again.

So here we have a very positive book on sewing machines, it is also practical and cuts through the technical jargon and terminology.

THE SEWING MACHINE in this book will be looked at objectively. It could be of many makes although it will be necessary to refer to some special features on individual machines. Hopefully by elaborating on what stitches, techniques and 'features' are hidden away inside machines in general it will help you understand just why a modern machine is a desirable thing to use . . . just why it is a help to have a range of stitches . . . just what you do get for your money . . . why top-of-the-range is more sophisticated and costlier than basic machines . . . and it will show the things you will want to look for when buying a new model . . .

There are a huge number of machines on the market which are excellent value for money, are well made, have good guarantees and have an excellent range of stitches/techniques to cover a wide variety of work. Remember, that it is a PERSONAL choice and what appeals to one user will not necessarily appeal to another and do not be persuaded into a purchase just because it is 'like a friend's' – unless you have tried and tested your friend's machine first, of course.

Hopefully, when you have read through the pages and looked at the pictures and diagrams you will understand why all the stitches and techniques are there – the advantages of having 'more than just zig-zag'.

Hopefully, you will want to experiment with your own machine, trying out techniques and stitches that you have not used before.

Hopefully, if you are making a new purchase, you will not disregard a machine with a variety of stitches "because I'll never use them", because if you know what they are for and if they are EASY to use – you will!

A small but dedicated range of 'utility' stitches can now be found on very modestly priced machines. Just because there are, say, six stitches on a machine does not mean they are 'fancy' stitches . . . they are more likely to be 'working' stitches to help with construction/mending and day-to-day sewing tasks.

If you are going to do various types of sewing – as most sewing machine users do – you should aim to buy, at the very least, a mid-range model with some of the features mentioned within these pages PLUS a good range of stitches and techniques to help cope with a wide range of fabrics and projects. You need the variety, you need the stitch quality that comes with a 'quality' product – and it is a fact that if you can obtain the stitches EASILY you WILL use them more and more.

The quality obtained with top-of-the-range models is usually excellent and often exceptional . . . just like buying the 'top' car of your dreams! NO! You may never, ever use every single stitch and permutation – but what does it matter! Everything you could dream about stitching is there at your fingertips, everything possible is incorporated to make life easy, give free range to your creativity plus a superb stitch quality: if it takes the rest of your lifetime to try it all out . . . no matter, just think what fun you will have!

choosing your machines

A positive attitude right from the start will be helpful when choosing the machine. It is not easy to know what you want when you do not know what is available so it is a good idea to do some research into the various makes and models available by collecting leaflets and information from the shops. You can also send away to the manufacturers, via advertisements in magazines and newspapers, for information on their products and a list of stockists. You can also read reviews in magazines and detailed publications such as this one!

Although you may in due course, purchase the same make of machine that you own already, initially sift through all the information you can lay your hands on to compare just what you get for your money across the variety of machines available.

Price is one of the most important factors in your purchase and yes! you will get a more proficient model with a better stitch quality if you 'pay a little more': a cheap machine will sew an adequate seam, a more expensive machine will sew a good seam, a top-class machine will sew a perfect seam. You must not expect £1,000 performance from £100 machines.

Another 'hang up' with some prospective purchasers is that a comprehensive model with more than just the very basic utility stitches is a waste of money – 'they' will never be used. 'They' will if the stitches can be extracted from the machine easily with simple stitch selection and stitch width and stitch length controls. It is also often the case that the machines with the best stitch quality will be in the mid to higher range models: even if you never use the complete range of stitchery the standard of your stitches will be so good that it

Test, Try Use, Choose

is worth paying the extra for something you may rarely take advantage of.

The easiest machines to use are the computers but these are often ignored for two reasons. The first is one of price. It is assumed that they are expensive just because they are computerised despite the fact that the modest computers now start off in the same price range as mechanical and electronic models. The second is one of fear. Fear that they will break down more easily and fear that the user will not be able to manage it. They won't – and they will! More on computers later, but they are tried and tested and have been out for many years now, they are as reliable as a colour TV and a home computer. They are so easy to use that if the person behind the controls will just relax and approach the machine as they would a new microwave or similar item their fears would just melt away.

At Point Of Purchase

Test pieces

Having done your homework you will arrive in the shop prepared to make your purchase. Take a list of the things that you KNOW you want on your new machine: our check lists later in the chapter will help you. Also take pieces of fabric from your remnant bag along with you for test pieces but do allow the demonstrator to show you the stitchery on firm cotton fabric first. (You will understand more fully the sense of this when the value of 'doodle cloth' is covered in the next chapter.)

Trying the controls

Ask to see the basic/utility stitches not just the decorative ones and insist on seeing the buttonhole system – or systems if there is more than one way, as there often is. If you are looking at a machine with the motif embroidery systems/attachments see these working too – BUT – don't be fobbed off with just seeing the embroidery system with a comment such as "and the machine does normal stitching too". Removing the embroidery unit/frame should be simple to perform and it is important that you can manage it without confusion: try doing it yourself. You also need to see the machine performing 'normal' sewing, of course!

Use it yourself

Whatever machine your are reviewing, you MUST use it yourself. Try moving the knobs, levers, dials and so on as some are physically easier to move than others. If it is a machine controlled by a sensor 'touch' LCD panel, make sure you understand the method and can actually do it. This is a simple system but again, it can be confusing if you have not come across it before.

Additionally, you MUST use the foot pedal yourself. There are thick ones and thin ones, some take the whole foot on board, others just your toes: some are best used with bare feet and others with a heeled shoe. You need to be comfortable with this control more than any other . . .

The foot pedal should make smooth adjustment to the speed of stitching and provide an immediate response. Sew fast and sew slowly to judge your control over the needle: one-stitch-at-a-time control by a slight touch on the pedal is quite possible with computer machines and many electronic ones too. You need to check this out.

Some models have hand stop/start with a slider for speed control as an alternative to a foot pedal: try this yourself or any other method of hand control. If you are disabled or have problems chasing the foot pedal around the floor in the normal way, this could be extremely advantageous so check this out.

The final test . . .

Finally, in my experience a satin stitch is a good test of the stitch quality on ANY machine. Adjust the zig-zag stitch length to obtain a good close satin stitch (the method is described in the chapter on stitches): you may need to adjust the tension slightly to a lower than average number.

Types Of Machines

Machines of any make fall into different types and it is as well to take a look at this right at the beginning.

Mechanical machines

Mechanical machines work on a cam system. The more stitches there are the more cams you have, with a stacking system for lots of stitches.

The machine is used by adjusting a series of knobs or levers for stitch selection and width and length which 'lock' onto the cams. Machines are still in use where the cams are slotted into the machine each time a new stitch is selected but these days, the cams are usually built into the machine and will only be visible if the top is taken off for maintenance purposes.

Electronic machines

Electronic models are mechanical machines with electronic features and should not be confused with computers although these days they can have liquid crystal display (LCD) read-out information panels which can indeed be confusing on first glance.

The electronic features are usually in the foot pedal providing better control and needle penetration. Stitch selection can also have electronic features such as LED (light emitting diodes) lights indicating which stitch has been chosen.

Computer machines

Microchip technology has revolutionised sewing machines as it has other domestic equipment. With micro-chips, there are far less moving parts so there is less to go wrong! All stitch selection, programming, buttonhole memorising and stitch sequences etc. is done by computer control. All this is described in more detail in a later chapter.

Flat bed machines

Few flat bed models are bought these days although there are many hundreds of thousands still in use. Sturdy machines, they were often fitted into the old-style cabinets and sewing tables. Because of the advance in machine technology and production methods the following type is more popular.

Free arm machines

The very first free arm was developed in France in 1860! They did not come into modern use until about a hundred years later when they were daubed 'sleeve-arm machines' which graphically explains why they are so popular. The arm is built into the main body of the machine but the freedom to pull sleeves, trouser legs and other cylindrical items around them for ease of stitching is a marvellous boon to dressmakers. Sewing collars and cuffs, children's clothes and curved seams are all easier with the free arm and very basic as well as sophisticated ones can have this facility.

The free arm is not always apparent when glancing at a machine as all models will have some type of extension plate/area fitted on to give a larger area for stitching flat items. Some plates pull off/on, some slide off/on, some are complete boxes inside of which you can hide

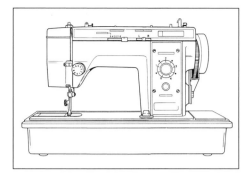

Flat bed machine

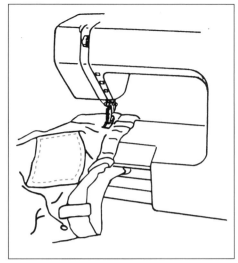

Free arm machine

away the accessories. Check out how easily it is to remove and replace the extension plate/area.

It should be noted that some free arms are slimmer than others and this varies from make to make and sometimes from model to model – if this is an important feature to you check it out.

Basic machines

Few people even desire a straight stitch machine these days, and if they do so for a special reason they will buy an old one, or perhaps an industrial model.

The basic zig-zag machine will be mechanical and the ability of the needle to swing from side to side will provide the zig-zag stitch alongside a straight stitch but no others. We will discuss zig-zag along with other stitches in a separate chapter: it is undoubtedly very useful but the ability of a machine to do other zig-zag-type stitches, such as tricot zig-zag, is advantageous.

Even if you want a relatively basic model do not just opt for the very bottom one without looking at the alternatives with a few extra stitches.

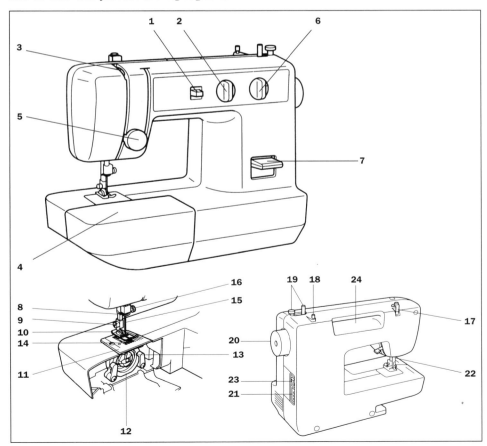

AN EXAMPLE OF A BASIC MACHINE WITH ALL PARTS SHOWN . . .

1 Needle position selector
2 Stitch width knob
3 Thread take-up lever
4 Extension table
5 Upper tension control dial
6 Stitch length knob
7 Reverse sewing button
8 Thread cutter
9 Presser foot screw
10 Presser foot
11 Needle plate
12 Shuttle hook
13 Bobbin case
14 Feed dog
15 Needle
16 Needle clamp screw
17 Thread guide/bobbin winding tension disc
18 Spool pin
19 Bobbin winding assembly
20 Balance wheel
21 Foot control plug socket
22 Presser foot lever
23 Main power/sewing light switch
24 Built-in handle

AN EXAMPLE OF A MID-RANGE AUTOMATIC MACHINE WITH ALL PARTS SHOWN . . .

1 Front (lamp) cover plate
2 Press-o-matic pressure control
3 Thread take-up lever
4 Bobbin winder tension/front thread guide
5 Fold-away carrying handle
6 Retractable thread spool pins
7 Bobbin winder spindle
8 Bobbin winder stop
9 Top plate
10 Balance wheel
11 Inner clutch wheel
12 Machine arm
13 Stitch length control
14 Reverse stitch control
15 Stitch selector control
16 free arm
17 Shuttle cover plate
18 Presser foot
19 Feed dog teeth
20 Needle plate
21 Presser foot holder screw
22 Needle bar
23 Needle clamp thread guide
24 Needle clamp screw
25 Tension unit
26 Centre thread guide
27 Zig-zag width dial

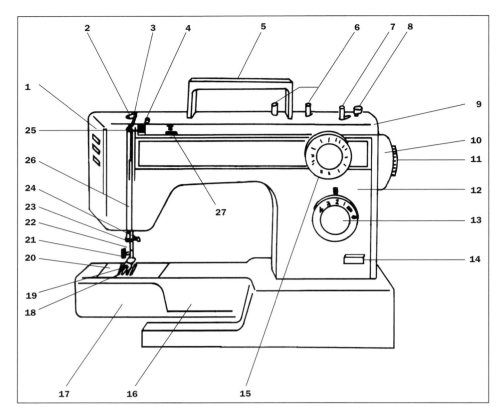

AN EXAMPLE OF AN AUTOMATIC MACHINE WITH ELECTRONIC FEATURES . . .

1 Bobbin winder device
2 Stitch length dial
3 Spool pin and spool holder
4 Stitch width dial
5 Upper tension control dial (automatic)
6 Light switch
7 Needle threader
8 Extension table & accessories compartment
9 Start/stop button
10 Reverse sewing button
11 Speed range control lever
12 Pattern selection dial
13 Power cord plug socket
14 Main switch
15 Controller jack for foot pedal
16 Buttonhole fine adjustment screw
17 Electronic display panel (LCD)

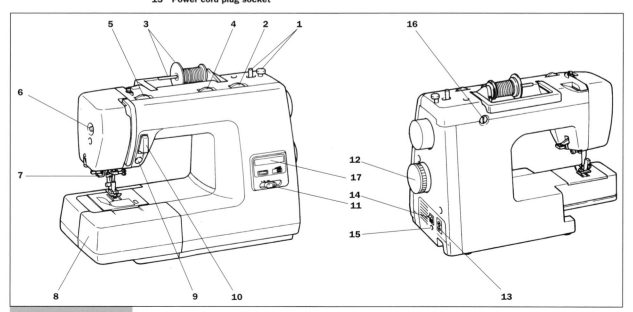

Mid-range automatic machines

Still mechanical, these machines will give a range of utility stitches including an easy buttonhole.

Utility stitches will include stretch stitches for seaming and overcasting and many will also give a range of decorative stitches too. The buttonhole may be 4-step, 5-step or progressively a 1-step and the systems do vary with some easier than others. If this is important to you check it out.

As you rise in capabilities and functions so too you rise in price.

Top range machines

The top of the mechanical range can be quite sophisticated in number of stitches and techniques with good-to-excellent stitch quality. They will usually have electronic features (as mentioned above).

The first computer models will come in at about the same price level, but here the choice may become difficult weighing up dozens of stitches with the electronic models against limited stitches with the basic computers for the same money!

The £500 mark (as we go to print) can be quite a watershed and the wide choice in this monetary area is greater than anywhere else in the price spectrum.

The computers will incorporate more and more with each rise in price but the basic computer ingredients remain the same regardless of the number of stitches: simple stitch selection where the stitch, width and length are all set together with just one control button, over-ride for personal preferences and stitch adjustment, excellent needle penetration, needle up/down by selection other than turning the balance wheel, memory facilities to hold your pattern combinations and lots more besides.

AN EXAMPLE OF A MID-RANGE COMPUTER WITH ALL PARTS NAMED . . .

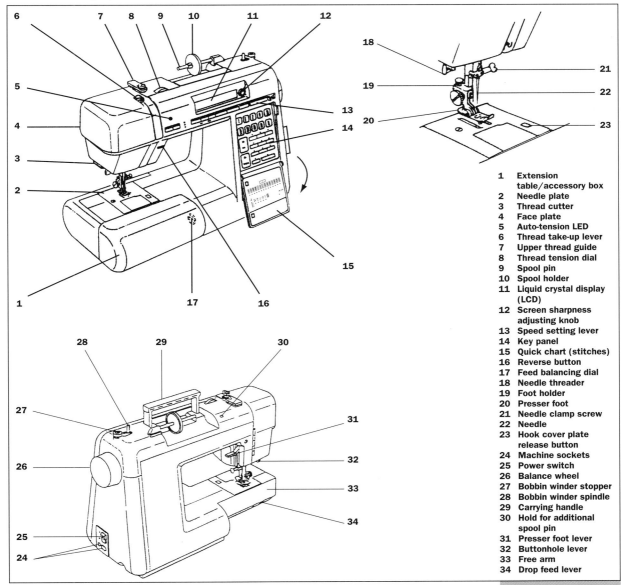

1 Extension table/accessory box
2 Needle plate
3 Thread cutter
4 Face plate
5 Auto-tension LED
6 Thread take-up lever
7 Upper thread guide
8 Thread tension dial
9 Spool pin
10 Spool holder
11 Liquid crystal display (LCD)
12 Screen sharpness adjusting knob
13 Speed setting lever
14 Key panel
15 Quick chart (stitches)
16 Reverse button
17 Feed balancing dial
18 Needle threader
19 Foot holder
20 Presser foot
21 Needle clamp screw
22 Needle
23 Hook cover plate release button
24 Machine sockets
25 Power switch
26 Balance wheel
27 Bobbin winder stopper
28 Bobbin winder spindle
29 Carrying handle
30 Hold for additional spool pin
31 Presser foot lever
32 Buttonhole lever
33 Free arm
34 Drop feed lever

AN EXAMPLE OF A TOP COMPUTER MACHINE WITH TOUCH SENSOR DISPLAY/CONTROL PANEL WITH ALL PARTS NAMED . . .

1 Handle
2 Thread guide for bobbin winding
3 Spool cap
4 Needle threader lever
5 Thread cutter
6 Buttonhole lever
7 Needle threader
8 Presser foot
9 Feed dog
10 Bobbin cover
11 Drop feed lever
12 Bobbin winder device
13 Balance wheel
14 Speed range control slider

A Main power switch & connectors
B Accessories compartment
C Selection key
D LCD. control panel
E Operation buttons: thread trim, needle up/down, reverse, stop/start button

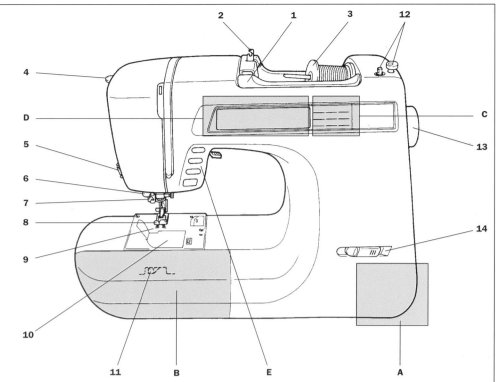

  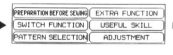  

UTILITY STITCH	BASIC SEWING	CARD & EMBROIDERY
CHARACTER SEWING	BASIC OPERATION	MEMORY
DECORATIVE STITCH	SEWING APPLICATION	STITCH ADJUSTMENT

PREPARATION BEFORE SEWING	EXTRA FUNCTION
SWITCH FUNCTION	USEFUL SKILL
PATTERN SELECTION	ADJUSTMENT

WINDING BOBBIN	CHANGING PRESSER FOOT
SETTING BOBBIN	CHANGING NEEDLE
UPPER THREADING	EMBROIDERY

Selection key and Liquid Crystal Display/touch control panel

THE MACHINE WITH EMBROIDERY UNIT IN PLACE . . .

1 On/off switch
2 Embroidery hopper foot
3 Unit connector
4 Memory card/smart card
5 Clear view bobbin
6 Hoop
7 Presser foot lever & stop/start button
8 LCD. display/control panel

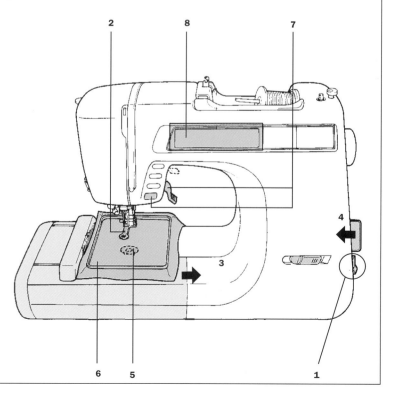

Making Your Sewing Easier . . .

The needle still goes up and down to make a stitch – so how can they have made sewing easier?

The answer is by making the controls easier and providing stitches to cope with the wide range of man-made and mixed fibres: machines can also contain a large number of sewing aids. You will see on our first Check List that everything is to do with making the machine work well for you. If you have not looked at machines for a while you may not even realise that some of these aids are available: alternatively you may well have some/all of these items and not realise OR not utilise them. Also, you do not necessarily spend a fortune to get some of the items many of which are on quite 'basic' models.

Easy threading is a boon! Mis-threading causes so many problems that the easier the machine is to thread the better. ALL machines are a lot easier to thread than they used to be, but true 'easy threading' is where the machine can be threaded in a twinkling with ONE HAND from top reel to needle – even the take-up lever, usually has a slit instead of a hole. The threading system is usually a numbered/lettered route and easy to follow. When you get to the needle, many machines have needle threaders that really do work! This must be one of the biggest boons in sewing today!

Easy bobbin threading is also a blessing. Drop-in bobbin systems are often easier to cope with than bobbin cases and are precision pieces of equipment. Using plastic bobbins and a drop-in bobbin ensures that you can see how much thread is left. There is an excellent quick-thread bobbin system available from Brother where the thread is taken through the circuit and just left . . . it is automatically picked up when stitching commences. Although the drop-in bobbin is, perhaps, easy to see there is nothing wrong with the front loading bobbin system – also precision engineering. The main thing to remember is to make sure it 'clicks' into position – if it slips the machine will not stitch. Many front loading machines incorporate a BOBBIN ALARM so that you know when the bobbin is running out. This can be a flashing light or even

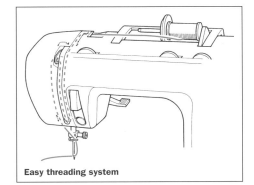
Easy threading system

a readout display BOBBIN RUNNING OUT! Top loaders in computer ranges will often have this too.

De-clutch bobbin winding. Instead of turning a disc inside the balance wheel to stop the machine from working whilst a bobbin is wound, the majority of machines now operate a system where the needle movement immediately cuts out when the winder is in operation. Quick, easy and accurate this is totally reliable.

Clip-on feet are a wonderful invention. Whilst it is accepted that most normal stitching tasks can be done with the basic foot, there are many reasons to want to change feet – zippers and buttonholes are but two examples. If you can clip feet on and off quickly and easily you are more likely to change the feet and use more techniques than when the machine uses screw-on feet.

The feet clip-on to an ankle piece – various manufacturers use different, but simple, systems. They are usually numbered or lettered for easy identification. Should you wish to use a screw-on specialist foot such as a ruffler or walking foot then the whole ankle piece will unscrew to allow the specialist foot to take its place. As you will see from the illustrations, the unique Bernina feet clip-on in a totally different way to other makes and it is a fact that Bernina supply more feet with machines than any other company.

Needle threaders are now quite common as built-in equipment and most of them really do work well. If this is an important feature to you DO TRY IT IN THE SHOP because some are easier than others – I particularly like the Pfaff/Janome/Brother/Frister systems.

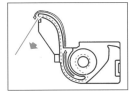
Quick-thread system from Brother

Front loading bobbin

Bernina feet clip on higher up

CLIP-ON FEET

Most models have a sprung lever or button system

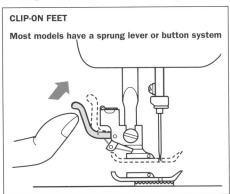

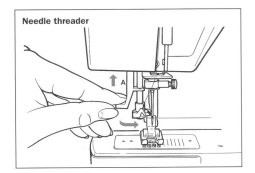
Needle threader

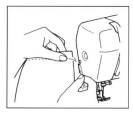

Thread cutter

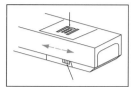

The Drop Feed lever position can vary from model to model

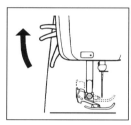

Double lifting of the presser foot for bulky articles

Thread cutters have been on machines for years – usually a 'slit-type' behind the needle clamp. They have improved! Most are now positioned so that the threads can easily be slipped through the cutter as the fabric is taken out of the machine: look up, to the left from the needle, on the back corner of the casing for the best position. (Bernina, Pfaff, Janome, Brother.) Look for a cutter beside the bobbin winder for the bobbin thread at the end of winding – very useful.

Free arm models are now the norm and the assets have already been noted.

Variable needle positions have also been around for a while: stitching to the left, right or centre position this facility is a boon for top and edge stitching, tucks and much more. Over the past few years, modifications have provided machines with more and more needle positions: they can now come in 10/15/20 or more rather than just the 3! Each position will be totally accurate for straight stitching – and do not scoff at this large number because I assure you that the more you have the more you use . . . and to excellent effect.

To drop feed dogs on some machines is a lot easier than others. Some models have an easy 'switch' or 'lever' in a convenient position – some in inconvenient positions! Some do not have a way of dropping the feed dogs at all – and to 'do away with the feed' you must cover the feed dog with a plate. You do not need 'feed' when you do free embroidery, free darning or stitch on a button. With motif sewing on some top-of-the-range models, the feed dogs will drop automatically when this type of stitching is selected. If you intend to do a lot of work without the feed you will probably find the lever method is easiest.

Rest assured though, that it IS POSSIBLE to do free embroidery, monogramming etc. without feed on ALL machines, including the computer models.

Double lift is on most machines – lurking unsuspected, very often! Try pushing up the presser foot lever to a secondary 'high' position thus making a bigger gap under the presser foot. This facilitates very thick cloth (such as heavy coating) to slide more easily into position under the needle. When you leave go of the lever, it will find its own natural pressure level. REMEMBER though, you must still 'drop' the lever before you sew, to engage the tension unit.

Automatic tension is now available on a huge number of machines. It is usually excellent for all normal stitching, embroidery etc. etc. on a wide range of materials. However, it is ALWAYS possible to manually adjust tension if you need to 'fine tune' it for specialist work!

Easy stitch selection is achieved in very many ways. Easy can mean two things – easy to manipulate – easy to achieve! Particularly if you have arthritic problems or other disabilities the EASE of altering/programming is important . . . however, even without disabilities EASE of selection is important because the easier it is to do, the more you will do! Undeniably, computer systems are the EASIEST because just the slightest touch of a button/picture on a window panel makes the alteration for you. With a mechanical machine, the EASE of turning a dial is important – try it in the shop! Some are easier to move than others.

EASY also means SIMPLE! Again, a computer machine has to be the easiest system. Touching a button/picture which automatically provides the selected stitch with the correct width and length in a couple of seconds is

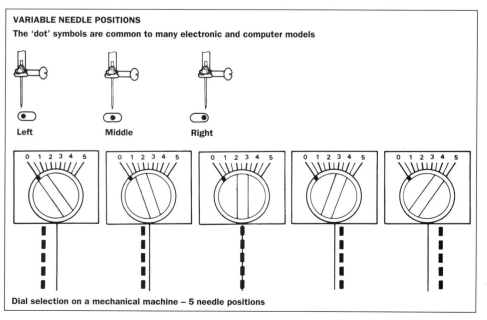

VARIABLE NEEDLE POSITIONS
The 'dot' symbols are common to many electronic and computer models

Left   Middle   Right

Dial selection on a mechanical machine – 5 needle positions

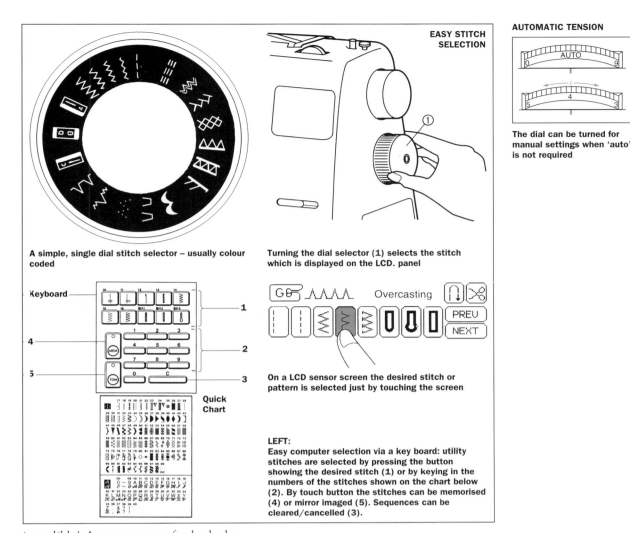

A simple, single dial stitch selector – usually colour coded

Turning the dial selector (1) selects the stitch which is displayed on the LCD. panel

Keyboard — 1
— 2
4 —
5 — 3

Quick Chart

GB ⋀⋀⋀⋀ Overcasting

PREV
NEXT

On a LCD sensor screen the desired stitch or pattern is selected just by touching the screen

LEFT:
Easy computer selection via a key board: utility stitches are selected by pressing the button showing the desired stitch (1) or by keying in the numbers of the stitches shown on the chart below (2). By touch button the stitches can be memorised (4) or mirror imaged (5). Sequences can be cleared/cancelled (3).

AUTOMATIC TENSION

AUTO
0   9

5   4   3

The dial can be turned for manual settings when 'auto' is not required

---

incredible! An easy system for both the novice and the experienced.

SIMPLE too, on a mechanical machine is the colour-coded-system whereby selecting the stitch, stitch length and stitch width can be done in 3-steps with colour-coded help on the dials. ONE-DIAL selection is even more SIMPLE and is an excellent type of first machine.

BEWARE OF THE OVER-SIMPLE if you are an experienced sewer. A few of the single dial methods of stitch selection mean that you cannot adjust the width of stitch and/or length because it is ALWAYS pre-programmed for you – if you are used to a variable machine this can prove quite a limitation. **You need to investigate each model because some single-dial machines are variable and some are not!** EASY/SIMPLE is what is "easy/simple" to your own brain no-one else's! Try out the various systems and see which one you prefer . . . there are lots on offer.

One-step buttonholes are undoubtedly the best kind to go for although there are various different methods available by different manufacturers. One-step can be mechanical or computerised: they can have sliding feet or sen-

J Zigzag Stitch

STITCH WIDTH W   STITCH LENGTH L   THREAD TENSION S
0.0 mm N   2.5mm S   AUTO   W

sor feet. At the lowest end of the ranges you may have 3-step which is a lot easier than the old basic method where you have to turn the fabric/garment around but if you do lots of dress/clothes then it is worth paying more for a really efficient one-step buttonhole! The various methods are discussed in more detail in a later chapter.

Lock off! Is not found on every machine but it is wonderful to have! Some models (Janome models and some Bernina) lock off on the spot (4/5 stitches) and others like the Pfaff do one or two reverse stitches. Elna/Bernina/Brother etc. will lock off at the end of some embroidery patterns and with motifs but not every machine will lock off with straight and zig-zag where you do need it to. 'Lock off' should not be confused with the automatic reversing at the beginning and end of a row of straight stitching which is

Left: The LCD panel shows the tension settings and any alteration is done by touching the sensitive screen.
S = stronger tension and W = weaker tension

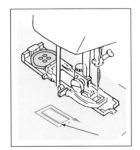

One step buttonhole system

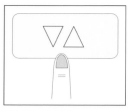

Two illustrations of popular symbols for Up/down needle control

built into some computer models – that is also excellent, but different.

Reverse EVERYONE KNOWS ABOUT REVERSE! but wait! Here is something to look out for . . . holding the reverse button for instant reverse is nothing new and is STANDARD on all makes and models. On some of the top machines, however, when you press reverse, they lock off. (Various makes). This is an asset to many degrees BUT if you actually want to reverse and NOT lock off, it is infuriating! In their wisdom, the automatic programmers (not 'sewers' I'll warrant!) have chopped off reverse on some quite ordinary stitches like tricot and other utility stitches where it is likely that you might want to go backwards . . . why have they done this? who knows! but if this is important to you it is a point to double check.

Special Things To Make Sewing Easier . . .

Here are some other things which are less common or are quite unusual – some protected by patent from another manufacturer using them! A few of the most helpful are listed below – you will obviously find other specialist items as you look around.

Up/down needle control came in with computers but is now available on mid-range machines too and will be found across the various manufacturers. For the needle to stop in the UP position is so helpful . . . it means that you can whip out the fabric when the machine stops without having to adjust the balance wheel to release the threads. Many machines by various manufacturers will now do this. However, it is not always required to take the fabric 'out' as you stop stitching. You may, for instance, want to turn a corner with the needle 'down'. Here the up/down comes into its own because by the mere quick press of a button – not by turning the balance wheel – the needle pops down into the fabric. GREAT! Press the button again and the needle pops up. When the machine does this, it means that you seldom need to adjust the needle height with the balance wheel ever again . . . with the up/down button immediately over the needle, it is quicker and easier to do this mundane little task that we have to do repeatedly during all our stitching. AN IMPROVEMENT ON UP/DOWN CONTROL

is found at the top of the ranges where the needle can be 'told' to stop-up-all-the-time or down-all-the-time until you tell it otherwise. This gives exceptional control in all very fine work where you are constantly lifting/dropping the presser foot to change direction.

Needle penetration on all makes of machines has improved dramatically with modern 'electronic' motors and tests on them and computer machines has been sometimes hard to believe. In some tests stitching 10 layers, or more, of heavy denim with a size 11 needle, for instance has proved quite easy! It is still recommended that you use the correct size needle to fabric for good stitch quality, but the point of excellent needle penetration is that the positive surge controlling the needle takes strain from the motor, needle and fabric. It is making sewing easier by taking the strain from the machine plus the sewer!

HELP! Mid-range machines are more and more likely to have read-out panels now that liquid crystal panels are being introduced into lower priced machines: and what a help they can be. As well as being able to see the chosen stitch displayed the length and width is shown too . . . if you vary any of the settings, it is immediately relayed to the display panel. The system is so

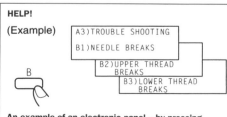

An example of an electronic panel – by pressing button B. the information appears in the LCD. window

Touching HELP! on the sensor screen will bring various options into view

simple, it is quite an easy step forward to enable the panels to HELP the user . . . some basic machines merely give guidance for stitch usage whilst others will actually roll-up a whole list of 'whys and wherefores' when you ask it for help. The degree of HELP varies through the price ranges, but at the very top you can have complete 'handbook' knowledge on-screen at the touch of a button . . . just like the home computer.

Hand control is in constant use now, with the sophisticated embroidery machines: whilst stitching the automatic motifs (with the hoops) only stop/start control is necessary. However, if you substitute 'no foot pedal' for hand control it tells another story. A number of makes (including Viking, Janome, and Brother) can work without the pedal which is a wonderful boon for the disabled as well as those who just find co-ordination with their foot/foot pedal is not easy! Viking have a head control (nod at the machine to make it work!) whilst Janome have a small control that tucks into the palm of the hand and plugs into the pedal socket. With Brother and various others, you merely unplug the foot pedal and use the stop/start button on the machine along with the slider speed controls. This feature is a definite plus for many people and should be investigated if you have any special needs or preferences.

Knee lift unique to Bernina for many years (although various industrial machines do have it too) it is now appearing on other makes. It is a great help when doing detailed, intricate work OR if you are a speedy stitcher working against the clock! Plugging easily into the machine, once in place a gentle push with the knee will lift the presser foot . . . after a surprisingly short time adjusting co-ordination you will find the knee lift surprisingly useful.

Dual feed is unique to Pfaff and is on all the top range machines and some of the mid-range too. The 'dual feed' pulls down into a slot in the presser foot and is thus working immediately over the feed dog: as you stitch, it acts as a feed dog from above, feeding the fabric through

DUAL FEED FROM PFAFF
The lever at the back pulls down between the sides of the presser foot to help with even feeding of the cloth

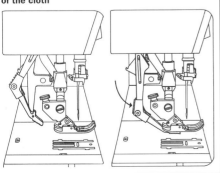

evenly. Designed for 'difficult' fabrics it is also a great aid to even stitching on a wide range of materials which are not particularly difficult – especially when you are top stitching.

If you do not have a Pfaff with a dual feed – the nearest thing to it is the walking foot!

Thread snips are one of the latest innovative ideas from Brother – although again, they have been on industrial machines for some years. The 'scissors' symbol is pressed and the 'underbed trimmer' (down with the bobbin) quickly snips the top and bottom threads when you take out the fabric. Lazy? Lazy! Like lots of other new features you may not think you want it – but once you have used it, you wouldn't want to be without it!

Memory/edit is the facility for the machine to remember your own various sequences of stitching – whether decorative or utility, or even a special buttonhole – as well as pre-programmed ones is available on most computers, but not necessarily the bottom range of computers. Editing is not always available even on top machines, but on some makes it is easily done: you do not always want to start again if a mistake is made in programming right at the beginning. If this is important to you CHECK!

Check Out The Accessories

Stow and go . . . home or away, the accessories are an important and integral part of the machine.

EVERY model has a range of accessories which include extra presser feet, screw driver, cleaning brush and other bits and bats depending on the sophistication of the machine. Some models stow the extra feet tidily and safely inside the 'head'/body of the machine whilst in others it can be quite common for the accessories to be stowed away inside a space in the free arm extension area. It will obviously keep them safer when integrated into the machine than those that have a little bag floating around. The safety factor is obviously more important if you move your machine around a lot, take it out to classes or even away on holiday. If this is particularly important to you, check it out.

The slider speed control is used in conjunction with the hand operated stop/start button

'THREAD SNIPS'
This automatic thread cutter button activates an under-bed trimmer to snip the top and bobbin threads and place the needle in its highest position to take out the work. It can be used manually as required or the instruction can be 'memorised' so that threads are snipped automatically at the end of a programmed sequence of stitching

STOW & GO
An example of an accessory box contained within the free arm extension table: feet are neatly stowed in their proper place in the removable tray and larger items (such as brush and screwdriver) sit in the box underneath

getting started

The modern sewing machine is a superb tool to give perfect and professional results every time . . .

Unfortunately, many owners do not master their chosen model sufficiently to make it a true extension of their own fingers. In this chapter we will explore the machine to get you started on the right road to proficient use of the machine. Now is the time to get the new machine out of the box or the unused one from the back of the wardrobe or the cupboard under the stairs!

First . . .
DON'T BE AFRAID OF IT! Many ladies – but not so often the men-folk – are very nervous of electrical appliances and technical machinery of any type and additionally, computers can strike terror into many hearts. It is also understandable that many who used old straight-stitch hand operated machines which had an electric motor added on and who found that the machines 'ran away with them', are still very nervous about controlling their new machines. Indeed this often happened with early electric machines too.

We need to overcome these fears by a feeling of confidence that will only come when you are really at ease with the machine and know it as well as you know yourself. Every knob, switch, dial, control panel, every setting for every stitch, every use for every presser foot should be familiar so that you do not need to hesitate every time you want to set it in motion.

There is only one way to get to know all this and that is to Practice with a capital 'P'! Practice can be fun and not a chore, so try to make this indispensable time a period of adventure rather than one of boredom. The more experimenting you do the more ideas come along and when you are getting ideas thick and fast you are enthusiastic to try more and more experimenting – it is an endless circle. It can also be fun to share ideas with friends who also like to sew and you will find that you all stimulate each other into new experiments.

Practice can be fun
Pedal = Good control
Threading = Good stitching
Good stitch formation =
A job well done

These are the positive and progressive steps to tread on your adventure of getting to know about your machine and making friends with it.

EVEN IF YOU HAVE USED THE MACHINE BEFORE, FOLLOW STEP BY STEP AS INDICATED – I guarantee you will discover at least one new thing about the machine, probably a lot more.

Step 1
If your machine is to become a true mechanical needle – an extension of your own hands – you must first master the control you have over it.

■ WITHOUT THREADING THE MACHINE attach the foot pedal, plug into the mains and turn it on.

■ Now, with the foot pedal, keep stopping and starting the machine (it will not damage it to run it in this way!) Learn how far down to press the pedal to get INSTANT needle movement.
With a mechanical machine, if you hear a buzzing noise then you need to push your foot down just a little harder. It is similar to taking up the gears on the car – you need to find the exact spot.
With an electronic machine you are unlikely to get this buzz and with a computer you definitely will not.

■ While you are doing this, observe where your needle stops: up, down or anywhere at all.

■ When you have mastered this then experiment with the speed of the machine: but do not just go very fast, go slow and see if you can do one-stitch-at-a-time. Electronic pedals and computers in particular should achieve this.

Step 2
Get out your instruction book that came with

Practice with the foot pedal

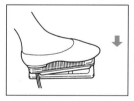

Lift the Presser Foot BEFORE you begin to thread

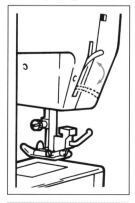

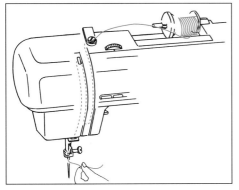

Practice threading and re-threading . . .

the machine and learn the threading routes on the top and the bobbin. These days, even very basic models will have an EASY THREADING SYSTEM which can be colour coded or numbered for you to follow. **THE BASIC THREADING ROUTE IS ALWAYS THE SAME NO MATTER WHAT MACHINE YOU OWN: from thread reel pin (which can be vertical or horizontal), via a slot or number of 'thread guides' to the tension, then another slot or 'thread guide' to the take up lever, and then via a slot or more 'thread guides' to the needle.**

▓ Use a good sewing thread for top and bobbin – there is more about threads in a later chapter.

▓ BEFORE YOU BEGIN to thread, lift the presser foot lever to release the pressure on the tension discs so that when the thread passes through the tension it will slip easily into place. Even if you have a slot threading machine and you cannot actually see the tension discs, they are there! If you need to lower the presser foot before you actually thread the needle, you should thread with the foot up.

▓ Now, practice threading time and time again . . . it should become a habit and be completely familiar to you.

▓ DON'T RUSH: more problems occur because a machine is mis-threaded than any other reason and even when you are totally familiar with the machine, it is possible to mis-thread in haste! A mis-thread around the top circuit will become apparent when you start to sew and long loops of thread appear UNDERNEATH the fabric. If this does happen, just un-thread the machine and re-thread it again.

BREAKDOWN OF THE EASY-THREADING SYSTEM

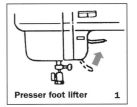

Presser foot lifter   1

Upper thread guide

2

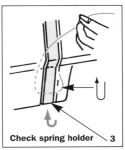

Check spring holder   3

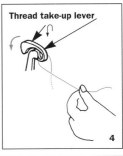

Thread take-up lever

4

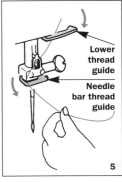

Lower thread guide

Needle bar thread guide

5

WINDING THE BOBBIN

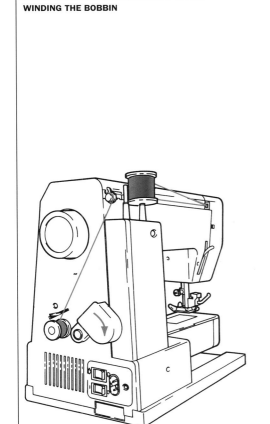

A mechanical machine and/or one with a vertical spool pin may have the bobbin on the side or on the top during winding

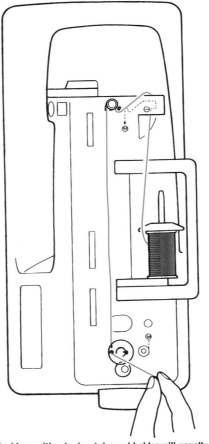

Machines with a horizontal spool holder will usually wind the bobbin on the top

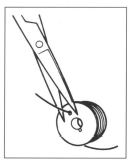

Clip off the 'tail' before you put the bobbin into the machine!

▨ Now wind a bobbin and insert it into the machine first raising the needle to its highest point. Check that there is not a little 'tail' dangling from the beginning of the wind, if there is just clip it off. Leaving a 'tail' could stop the bobbin from working smoothly.

▨ The bobbin will go into the machine via a bobbin case or drop straight into the race way in a top-loading model. Check the illustrations on whichever sort you have. Whether you put the bobbin into a bobbin case or directly into the bobbin-holder of the raceway, it is most important that the thread pulls against the tension spring – when you pull the thread it will seem to come back on itself when threaded correctly. When putting the bobbin into a bobbin case, the thread will USUALLY pull out in a clockwise direction as the bobbin faces you . . . but not exclusively so.
The latest top loading machines usually have the threading route printed on the cover plate, if not, then the instruction book will clearly show it.
Usually, the thread will pull off the bobbin in an anti-clockwise direction, but not exclusively so. Again, check it is through the tension spring.

▨ When you have loaded the bobbin into the case or the holder you should experience some tension when you pull the thread, if it pulls out easily it is either mis-threaded or in later use, the spring has worked loose and it needs adjustment via the little screw holding on the spring.

▨ Thread and re-thread over and over again until you are completely familiar with the system.

Bring up the bottom thread . . .

▨ With a non-computer, hold the tail of the top thread and turn the balance wheel a full circle, pull up the bottom thread by pulling the top one.

▨ With a computer, take one stitch with the foot pedal instead of turning the balance wheel, or alternatively use the needle up/down button. When you get used to this, you will find that doing it this way is quicker than turning the balance wheel . . .

Step 3

Now you will need some fabric to begin sewing. For testing a machine and experimenting you will need some 'doodle cloth'! You can either use some reasonably firm sheeting-type material or buy some of the demo. cloth that a store demonstrator uses – some companies will sell this to the public direct.
    The reason for using this type of cloth will be explained at the beginning of the chapter of Stitches.
    With the fabric double, start with a line of straight stitches and sew up and down on various stitch lengths to observe the differences.

▨ Search for a control to alter your needle positions and try them out . . . more on this in the Stitches chapter. For now just find the variety of positions available to you and see how they work.

▨ At this time, try reverse stitching too and make sure you know how your button or lever works, these can be in various positions on the machine. It is usual for

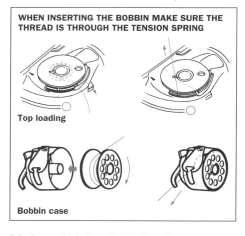

WHEN INSERTING THE BOBBIN MAKE SURE THE THREAD IS THROUGH THE TENSION SPRING

Top loading

Bobbin case

Bringing up the bottom/bobbin thread

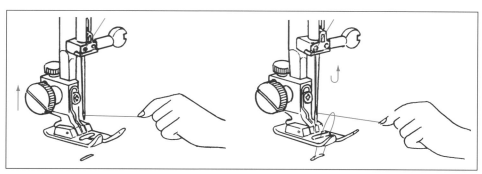

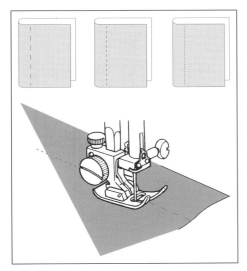

Start with straight stitch . . .

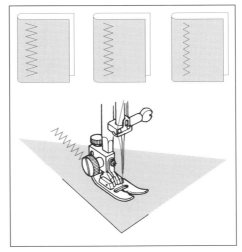

. . . and work on to zig-zag

the button to be held 'in' or lever 'down' whilst stitching backwards. Each time you try out a new stitch see what happens when you touch/activate reverse because on high range models other functions may also be utilised by 'reverse' on selected stitches.

When you are happy with straight and reverse, move on to zig-zag.

We now have two courses of action: one is for mechanical machines and the other for computers.

If you have a computer, try out zig-zag and then move on through the range of stitches, selecting, stitching and reversing and having fun seeing what happens each time. AT THIS STAGE, DO NOT OVER-RIDE ON ANYTHING! Just see the amazing amount of sewing that you can do 'straight from the brain' of the machine. Leave buttonholes for the time being.

When you have done that, re-join my suggestions below, using your over-ride facilities i.e. your ability to manually adjust the stitch width and length. This could be by dials, buttons or sensor touch panel.

If you have a mechanical model select zig-zag and experiment with the stitch width, then move on to the stitch length and zig-zag with wide open stitches and very close ones – this will give you a satin stitch. (More on this in the Stitches chapter.)

▪ Now move on through the range of stitches: this is the time to work out your colour coding if you have it – one type of setting for close (satin-stitch type) stitches and another for stretch or 'open' stitches.

▪ If you have a machine with a readout panel it will be similar to colour coding, but ask 'assistance' each time and see what

feet it suggests you should use, and recommended stitch widths and lengths.

When you have tried out the stitches as the manufacturer recommends (mechanical OR computer) start trying them on alternative widths and lengths – there are only a handful of machines that cannot be altered and have 'fixed stitches'.

▪ Observe the vast difference, particularly with a decorative or 'craft' stitch, between a wide and narrow stitch width particularly now that some machines stitch at a width of 9mm or even more. The same stitch on '3' wide and '9' wide will look totally different . . . then try altering the stitch length. This can adulterate the stitch to be totally unrecognisable – but try it just to see what happens! (More on this in the Stitches chapter.)

When you are happy that you understand how these controls work and the results that you get you can move on.

REACH INTO THE 'BIT-BAG' that every sewer has and come out with some different fabrics, from thick to thin. Now work through the stitches again and you will find very interesting things happening. The thick or heavy fabrics will react well to wide stitches and the fine or thin ones will not . . . not without help anyway.

DO NOT REACH FOR THE TENSION if a wide stitch puckers the thin fabric – it is not a tension problem, the pull of the thread is just too much so the machine re-acts differently. You know the tension is OK because you have just tested the stitches on firm fabric! Make the stitch narrower and the stitch will probably be fine. (More on this in the Stitches chapter.)

If you have pieces of leather and other seemingly extreme fabrics available, try these

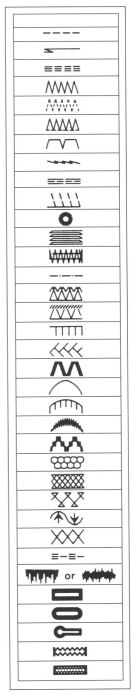

Work through the other stitches/patterns leaving the buttonholes until last

Key:

● & ▬ LED indicator lights
29 Stitch panel selector switch
15 – 28 Decorative stitches
30 Presser foot indicator
31 Needle stop down
32 ½ speed
33 Reverse sewing (continuous)
34 Single pattern or complete pattern and stop
35 Mirror image
36 Buttonhole
37 Long stitch (tacking)
38/39 Balance
40 Memory
41 Clear/cancel

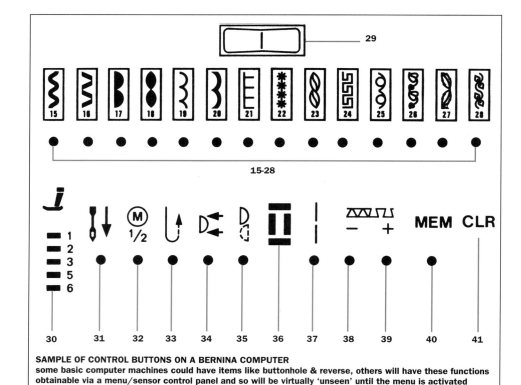

SAMPLE OF CONTROL BUTTONS ON A BERNINA COMPUTER
some basic computer machines could have items like buttonhole & reverse, others will have these functions obtainable via a menu/sensor control panel and so will be virtually 'unseen' until the menu is activated

too. Even try to embroider on leather – 99% of machines will, and do it well!

Finally, test your computer by trying VERY thick fabric under your needle: the penetration will amaze you and up to 10 or more layers of denim (or similar) should be the norm.

When you have come to understand the stitchery in the machine move on . . .

Start with your buttonhole system(s) and then try out every single control button on the machine, either 'blind' i.e. trial and error, or hand in hand with your instruction book or computer 'menu'.

DO NOT PRESUME ANYTHING! no matter what your old machine did, or what you think you do or do not know about the one that has been in the cupboard all this time, go through this testing process and I KNOW you will find things you did not know you had!!!

Keep practising . . .

A lot of the features you have found will be covered in depth under STITCHES or TECHNIQUES in a later chapter where I will explain when you want to use these things.

Use this method of 'playing' with the machine in an enjoyable sewing session, so that you will be familiar with the alternatives and know exactly how to expect your stitches and other controls to behave when you actually come to use them in sewing projects.

getting started

stitches and their uses

I t is amazing how many people still ask why they would benefit with more than just straight stitch and zig-zag!

Making the needle 'zig-zag' from side to side was merely the first step in modern machine development opening the way for more intricate stitches including the eventual development of backward-and-forwards motion of the feed dog in conjunction with needle movement – this is how 'stretch' stitches of all types are made.

The term stitch is used widely to denote various end results. Thus a label 'stitch' can denote anything from a series of stitches in a straight line to a number of stitches in quite complicated stitch formation with a general term, e.g. feather stitch, tricot stitch.

To complicate matters, some machine companies may call the same stitch formation a pattern – and having called it a pattern they may then call it by a completely different name. This is notable between European and Japanese companies and happens frequently in multi-language instruction books.

For example, 'overlock' is a patented name despite the fact that it is used so often to describe various stitches that perform this particular function such as overcast, overedge and so on.

There are also stitch terms crossing those of techniques: for instance 'blind hem' is a stitch sequence, but it is also a technique with a specialist presser foot.

To try and bring some order to a description of stitching, in this chapter are listed machine stitches (stitch patterns or stitch sequences) and their most common names, with alternative names where known.

In a later chapter will be listed techniques, and the same names may be used again if necessary e.g. the example just given of 'blind hem'.

Stitch width & stitch length govern each and every stitch in the machine except for pre-programmed motifs

Utility, Craft and Decorative . . . The right stitch for the right job . . . a 'technique' is what you do with that stitch – often with the help of a specialist foot.

Examples of adjusting stitch width and length: many machines now have 9mm stitch width. When straight and/or zig-zag are combined with backwards and forwards motion they produce stretch stitches and intricate patterns

Straight stitch

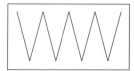

Zig-zag

Outline zig-zag

Tricot zig-zag

Ric-rac

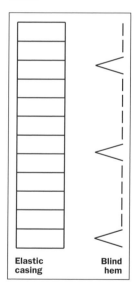

Elastic casing   **Blind hem**

Utility Stitches

Utility stitches are 'working stitches' used for construction and 'putting things together'...

Straight stitch

Use it to hold two or more fabrics together, as in seams, darts, tucks, pin tucks, top stitching, narrow hem, rolled hem, quilting, gathering, edge stitching and patchwork.

▪ On our modern machines, straight stitch can usually be sewn at the left, centre or right of the presser foot, and often with even more variations of position as some computers have been known to have upwards of 20 needle positions.

Zig-zag

The basic zig-zag stitch can be adapted by the user for many tasks.

▪ It is the accepted and original over-edge, neatening stitch and will still be used for this on basic models.

▪ It has been superseded by many better alternatives on machines with a choice of stitches.

▪ As with all patterns which incorporate stitch width, the ACTUAL width is crucial. With pre-set models and computers it will automatically come out 'wide' but do over- ride/adjust to make it narrower if any sort of puckering or bad stitch formation occurs.

▪ Zig-zag can be used in a multitude of width and length permutations on all fabrics to over-edge, appliqué and stitch over cords and braids (couching), to apply shirring and other fine elastics, to appliqué and attach lace, and with the twin needle.

▪ When the stitch is adjusted to a very low number on the stitch length so that the stitches lie closely side by side, this is called **SATIN STITCH**. On a computer, this can be achieved manually on 'over-ride' after programming the basic zig-zag stitch.

Outline zig-zag

Careful scrutiny will show this to be different from standard zig-zag.

Instead of diagonal stitch penetration, here two small stitches are taken side by side. The machine then moves forward to the next pair of stitches, and so on.

The zig-zag thus created is 'Z' shaped. This is a very narrow stitch (usually automatically set at '1' wide) and should be used on bulked fabrics where that width will be lost in the bulk of the fibres.

▪ It is an alternative to straight stretch stitch for stretch towelling, stretch velour, Crimplene-type fabrics and knitwear. It is a very stretchy stitch.

Tricot zig-zag

(multiple zig-zag, multi-stitch zig-zag, three-step zig-zag, elastic stitch)
Designed as a stretch zig-zag, this stitch can (and SHOULD!) replace basic zig-zag on many occasions. It is much better to overcast an edge with this stitch as it is firmer and flatter and holds more fibres in place. Use it, too, where you want strength and/or stretch.

▪ Apply elastic with this zig-zag on lingerie or children's wear for elasticated cuffs, ankles and waistlines.

▪ For an extremely firm and efficient darn run backwards and forwards over the damaged or slit area with this stitch using forwards and reverse. It is advisable to place a small piece of interfacing or lining fabric behind the darn to give added strength if the fabric has worn thin.

▪ Various darn sequences are available on computer machines but this stitch is an alternative: note that on a just a few computers tricot cannot be used in reverse – pushing the reverse button just locks it off!

Ric-rac

(stretch triple zig-zag)
This stitch is designed to sew high stretch fabrics such as Lycra for swimwear and underwear, and to repair or join elastic. It is used extensive in the ready-to-wear industry for these products.

▪ It is also an effective top stitch if used quite narrow.

Elastic casing

This is to sew over, and make a casing for, an elastic strip, such as knicker elastic. Ensure that the side stitches are just over the edges of the elastic. The stitch is ideal when used for wrists and ankles on children's wear and has various uses in craft-work.

▪ The stitch is also widely used with a wing needle in Heirloom sewing for decorative purposes.

Blind hem

This stitch is used to turn up hems on garments and curtains.

▪ The stitch will also give a shell tuck or shell edging on fine fabrics but the top tension will need to be increased slightly.

(For the techniques used, see chapter 5.)

Stretch blind hem
(zig-zag blind stitch)
Use it as for the previous stitch on stretch fabrics.

Flat lock
(closed overlock, stretch overlock)
This is designed to sew overlapped seams, binding or elastic on to woven and elastic/stretch fabrics. The stitch can be suitable as a 'seam and neatening' process to give a double stitched edge. Stitch on the seamline and trim away the excess seam allowance AFTERWARDS.

Straight stretch stitch
(re-enforced stretch, triple stretch, triple strength) This is the first of the stitches to incorporate the backwards-and-forwards motion of the feed dog . . . surprisingly, back-stitching will ALWAYS put stretch into a stitch (even a decorative stitch!).

■ Straight stretch is a particularly good stitch with double knits and stable knits, plush, velour, sports wear fabrics, Crimplene-type and other bulked fabrics.

■ Despite its name DO NOT use this stitch on very fine, silky jersey as it is too heavy and will pucker the fabric.

■ Because this stitch sequence includes a backstitch it is also very strong. Use when strength is required on denim, canvas, upholstery, trouser zips, crotch seams, arm holes, bags and hold-alls.

■ If there is no specially formulated saddle stitch on the machine, this stitch can substitute as a top stitch to good effect. Use it with one or two sewing threads (thread two strands as one through the top threading system and use one needle), or a bold buttonhole twist (here leave the normal sewing thread on the bobbin).

Knit stitch
(overlock, serge)
This is an all-in-one operation to provide a seam and neaten the edges, and is designed for knitted and stretch fabrics. It is, however, often suitable on various other materials.
   (Serge is the American term for overlock.)

Stretch overlock
As the name implies, this provides a stretch seam and neatens in one operation.

Double-edge zig-zag
This is an excellent seam and over-edge finish on fabrics that tend to fray a lot, such as linen and gabardine. Two zig-zags are simultaneously worked over the fabric edge.

Overlock
(professional overlock)
This provides a seam, a zig-zag over-edge and a chain or purl of threads off the edge between the zig-zag stitches. It simulates various commercial overlock finishes and that of the domestic overlocker, but it should not be confused by that type of 3/4/5-thread stitching.

Top Of The Range Machines May Have A Wider Selection . . .

Included with the range of Utility stitches you may find the following

Lock-a-matic
The machine will automatically do a number of reverse stitches for securing the beginning and ends of a seam.

Bar Tack
A strengthening 'tack' for pocket tops, pleats, bag handles and similar items. The machine will do two or more rows of stitching and then a satin stitch over the top. Sometimes pre-set length, sometimes adjustable.

Darn
The machine will do a sequence of stitching to effect a small, neat darn. Usually this sequence can be adjusted in size to the stitchers requirements.

Eyelet
Elna, Bernina and Pfaff have provided eyelet plates for many years for mechanical machines. In these days of computers, most of the top makes/models will perform an eyelet by merely pressing a selector button. Some machines will do a variety of sizes.

Tacking/Basting
It is fascinating to watch a match tack! Adjustments can be made to stitch/tack length usually, and the machine skips along with the needle doing a stitch every so often . . . there are various ways of tacking on various makes – but all are quick and easy.

Lateral and Directional Stitching
Major companies have perfected this to enable

Stretch blind hem

Flat lock

Straight stretch

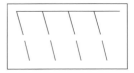
Knit stitch

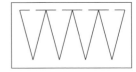
Stretch overlock

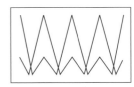
Double-edged zig-zag

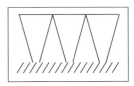
**Overlock
(professional overlock)**

Bar tack	Darn	Eyelet	Tacking	Directional stitching		
▨	‖‖‖‖ ‖‖‖‖ ‖‖‖‖ ‖‖‖‖	●	｜ ｜	– – – – → ← – – – –	⋎⋎⋎→	←⋎⋎⋎

Lock-a-matic

29

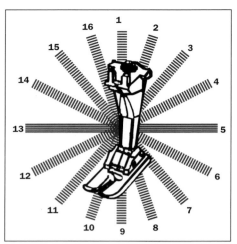

the machine to literally stitch sideways – or off on some other tangent – at the touch of a button. This can be amazingly useful for utility stitching in difficult places and it can also be incorporated into decorative sewing.

Craft Stitches

These stitches are often listed alongside utility stitches, but it is helpful to differentiate as they are usually decorative as well as utilitarian.

Feather stitch
This is usually an excellent copy of the hand embroidery stitch!

- Use it for patchwork and faggotting and other decorative work.

- It is an extremely stretchy stitch, and so is ideal to use on elasticated lingerie items, swimwear and knitwear.

- Because the formation is basically that of the straight stretch stitch – but with zig-zag width! – it is also very strong. Use it on domestic items, upholstery and luggage when a strong but more decorative than utilitarian finish is required.

Smocking stitch
This is a decorative stitch to give a smocked appearance. It is particularly useful on children's wear and lingerie. In fact, various other stitches can be used for smocking as well.

Paris point
Although in diagrams this often looks like an over-edge stitch, it is executed differently so try not to confuse the two!

- Paris point is a decorative hem stitch for household linens and it can look particularly effective when sewn with a wing needle.

- Use this stitch as well, to very good effect, incorporated into Heirloom sewing.

Honeycomb
This is a variation on 'smocking stitch' and can be used in the same way: also suitable for various finishes on lingerie and linings.

Scallop stitch
This forms a scallop shape made with STRAIGHT running stitches. The width and length of the scallop can be adjusted on many machines (but not all!) by adjusting the stitch width and length control.

- It can be used for a hem in dress or, collars and cuffs and for curtains and blinds. The three steps are stitch, trim and turn.

- It can also provide a superb scallop edge on a single layer of fabric for frills and collars in dress and as a finish for house hold linen, as follows . . .
  Sew around the edge of the item concerned with the scallop stitch placing the edge of the presser foot on the edge of

Scallop stitch

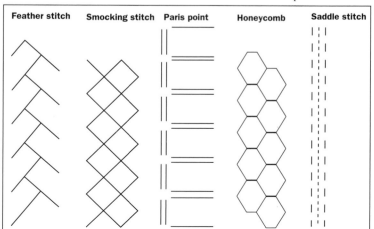

Feather stitch	Smocking stitch	Paris point	Honeycomb	Saddle stitch

the fabric as a guide to keep you straight. Then, using the stitching line as a guide, stitch over the top with a satin stitch. Trim the edges very close to the stitching afterwards with sharp scissors.

Saddle stitch
Saddle stitch or a sequence of saddle stitches can vary in appearance, but they are designed to perform the same task – a pronounced top-stitch line for dress.

■ It can also provide an effective heavy straight line for various uses in crafts, including quilting.

Blanket stitch
Designed for appliqué work, this is a more decorative finish than the basic zig-zag stitch and it has the appearance of its hand-sewn equivalent.

Herringbone
Use this for faggotting and general decorative stitching.

Greek key
This stitch is also used for faggotting and general decorative stitching.

Vine stitch
A decorative stitch which is extremely stretchy and suitable for finishing hems on fine jersey fabrics.

Decorative And Embroidery Stitches

Pre-programmed/selected decorative and embroidery stitches fall into two main groups: satin stitch and open stitch.

Decorative/embroidery stitches, call them what you will – they are usually extremely pretty and can be used in literally hundreds of ways. Note that some machines have literally hundreds of these types of stitches and by the time you have mixed/altered stitch length and stitch width the permutations for decorative work is truly amazing. Remember too, that by using the twin needle you can effectively double the number of stitches you have and even the very basic utility stitches can look attractive when it is used.

SATIN STITCH PATTERNS are solid patterns. OPEN STITCH PATTERNS are much more spidery/delicate in appearance.

■ There is often confusion about how to obtain the patterns: for the satin stitch type you MUST make the stitch length very short – nearly '0' – just as with ordinary zig-zag satin stitch.

■ The open stitch patterns are usually stitched with a very long stitch length OR with the machine set on stretch stitching,

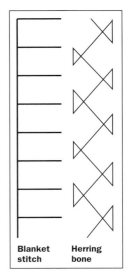

Blanket stitch | **Herring bone**

Greek Key | **Vine Stitch**

A SAMPLE OF STITCHES FROM JANOME.
It illustrates clearly the difference between open patterns and block (satin stitch) patterns.
56, 87 & 97 are examples of 'scroll patterns'.
71 is an example of a single cross stitch pattern.
The single pattern on the right-hand side, illustrates 'single pattern stitching' on a computer: when a stitch/pattern is put into memory, this is the portion that counts as '1-memory'.
Computer selection (on any make) will always start a pattern at the beginning – illustrated here by ○

If you are using these stitches on a non-computer machine and wish to start at the beginning of the design, it is necessary to set the pattern and count the stitches through whilst using doodle cloth BEFORE starting to stitch on the project in hand.

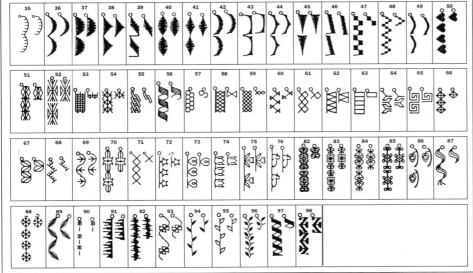

stitches and their uses

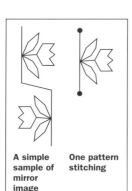

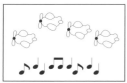

A simple sample of mirror image   **One pattern stitching**

Pattern elongation – the pattern is enlarged without destroyed the satin stitch

Motifs memorised with directional stitching between each design

Samples of alphabets with an embroidery unit

depending on the make and model you are using.

◻ Computer machines, of course, do the thinking for you and automatically set the machine correctly!

Scroll patterns

These are extremely intricate embroidery sequences combining both some satin stitches and reverse stitches – most of them are designed for borders but some computers have a selection of large scroll designs for motif use.

Cross-stitch

This is certainly embroidery however, one cross-stitch is not particularly attractive by itself! Rows of stitches are aligned to form a design: the stitch sequences can be for just one 'cross stitch' or for a variety of permutations on the theme in ones, twos or more.

Hem stitching

There is quite a variety of these stitches and some companies list them with utility stitches, others with craft, and others with embroidery.

The decorative quality of the stitches is enhanced by the use of the wing needle which is discussed in the Needles and Threads chapter.

Stitch sequences

Once obtained, the stitch will reproduce itself ad infinitum on a mechanical machine and until 'told' otherwise on a computer.

◻ The ability to memorise stitch patterns and sequences of your own choice gives great versatility to computer machines, allowing amazing scope in stitch mixing. The only way to discover the permutations of a machine is to experiment on it!

Mirror image

Most computers, but not all have the facility to mirror or 'turn over' the stitches. As well as 'turning over' the stitch some machines will turn/mirror it end-to-end and some will do both. If this is important to you, CHECK before you make a purchase.

◻ Note that you can mirror image utility stitches as well as decorative ones.
The variations can be very interesting, and basic or utility stitches mixed in with decorative or embroidery stitches produce

surprising results. When you are experimenting, therefore, it is useful to mix anything and everything together to see what happens and if you have lateral stitching too, it can be quite mind boggling!

One-pattern/stitch selection

Some computer machines will allow you to programme just one pattern and the machine will stop when that pattern is complete. Sometimes the machine will lock off automatically, sometimes you programme it to stop and lock off. Programming one pattern at a time allows a motif to be constructed, or details to be inserted here and there into a design, or maybe just one arrow-head or bartack in dressmaking.

Stitch elongation

This is another computer 'trick': the desired stitch/pattern can be elongated, sometimes to many times the original length, without distorting the stitch length or shape of the design.

Motif patterns

A lot of top range machines will do one-off patterns within their normal scope of stitching i.e. NOT with the aid of an Embroidery unit/hoop facility. This can be tiny 7-9mm on some or up 50mm or more. Often the size can be altered slightly and the machine will lock-off at the end.

Alphabet sewing

The majority of computer machines perform alphabet and numerical stitching which used to be considered a gimmick until so many mums found it super for name tags! There are of course many uses and with the memory facility complete names and addresses can be stitched out quickly and easily.

◻ At the bottom end of the ranges, letters can be done in capitals and/or lower case depending on the model. As you go up the range the combination of different types of alphabet will be incorporated giving the option of script or block, and eventually 'Old English' and various other fonts.

Monogramming

Large size lettering is somewhat different . . .

◻ Most of the major embroidery machines will do large monograms in a variety of styles without the aid of the hoop extension, some of them utilising the facility for lateral stitching. These can be up to 50mm in size.

◻ Those with Embroidery attachments or other type of large scale Embroidery units/hoops also do extra large letters via

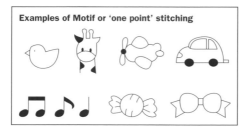

Examples of Motif or 'one point' stitching

their smart cards and with this facility they are most impressive.

- Including a surround for a monogram, badge style, is another feature that is proving extremely popular and the letters themselves can often be stylised and shaped for even more decorative effect.

Pictogram

This is a yet another computer machine technique but as this book goes to print it is unique to Viking. A series of pre-programmed stitch sequences can be chosen in any combination and programmed into memory by the operator to provide embroidered pictures or motifs.

Memory cards/Smart cards

Despite the fact that many top-of-the-range models have a vast amount of stitchery pre-programmed, quite a lot of machines now have a 'smart card' facility to supply even more.

- Purchasing a card with designs of your liking rather than a huge range you may not need, is a very sensible idea. Themes of such cards can be Anniversaries, Sports activities, Animals, Christmas and so on.

- Empty smart cards can provide your own personal memory bank to store designs mixed or most often used: they can also be used with a scanner.

Scanner

A custom designed system which enables the user to scan pre-printed items, hand drawing and much more besides. The chosen item can be stitched out in many colours – just scan the design for each additional colour – and the system is quite simple to use. With an LCD display and 'mouse' technology, the ability to enlarge and reduce the design this is truly innovative stitchery.

Free Embroidery and Monogramming

A traditional form of free machine embroidery, in which the feed dog is dropped and the fabric is moved freely under the needle by the operator to create the designs rather than utilising those built into the machine.

All machines will do free embroidery, even the top loading machines and computers. It is necessary to alter the tension on the BOBBIN for a lot of decorative effects and for this reason many prefer to use the bobbin case rather than the drop-in top-loading types.

However, some top loaders are more easily adjusted for bobbin tension than others, so if it is an important feature for you, check it out in the shop.

Fabric usually needs some support during free stitching and it can be held tightly inside a hoop or with a backing fabric such as Stitch

and Tear, interfacing, dissolving fabric, vanishing muslin or similar depending on the project in hand. The use of the hopping embroidery/darning foot is becoming more and more popular for free stitching.

Top of the range embroidery is becoming even more of an art form and is extremely simple to do!

Some call it cheating, but anything that helps to make people creative and enjoy their sewing is very much to be welcomed.

The type of machine where the sewer sees everything on screen, can adapt and alter, move the design within the hoop – 'mouse-fashion' – is amazing to see, creative and (excuse the phrase) user friendly.

The machines also have scanners available to put your own designs onto the 'smart cards' and stitch your very own designs. There are many pre-programmed cards available and the manufacturers are constantly adding to them. (Brother, Elna, Bernina, Janome, Viking).

Then there are the machines that link to the home computer for even greater flexibility and creativity (Bernina, Pfaff, Viking.) Providing you are at home with your computer and your sewing machine there is no reason why anyone should not get to grips with this type of inter-active work.

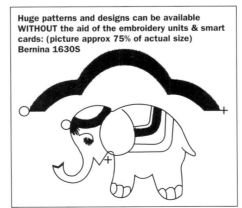

Huge patterns and designs can be available WITHOUT the aid of the embroidery units & smart cards: (picture approx 75% of actual size) Bernina 1630S

A monogram with pre-programmed border

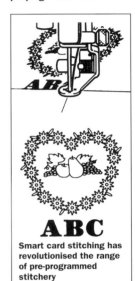

Smart card stitching has revolutionised the range of pre-programmed stitchery

Free embroidery shown without the foot and with a needle guard: the use of a hopper foot is a good alternative

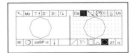

Designing on the screen 'mouse-style' with Bernina

33

buttonholes

Buttonholes can strike terror into machine stitchers!

The Bernina sensor buttonhole foot suitable for corded buttonholes – other companies have sensor feet too

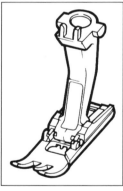

The Bernina 'basic' buttonhole foot, with grooves underneath. Note that there are no hooks for a cord

I used to put poppas or snaps on everything until I discovered automatic buttonholes! You may think that faint-hearted, but I am sure many sewers have done just the same.

The only way to do a buttonhole on a very basic machine is to stitch the first side and then TURN AROUND the fabric to do the second side – enroute you need to alter the stitch width twice to allow for the bar tacks and going back to the narrow stitches again. This is extremely simple to perform on a sample – but when the 'fabric' in question is a suit jacket and at the very least a shirt or blouse, this is just not as simple as it would appear.

There is no doubt that if you want to do dressmaking in any quantity AND quality! then you need some type of 'automatic' buttonhole. Hopefully, as you read on you will discover (as I did long ago) just what a modern miracle this is: not only that 'it' exists but there are in fact, a VARIETY of 'automatic' buttonholes.

Look around these pages and you will see various diagrams of buttonholes and feet. There are so many alternatives – some models do some, some another, and sometimes machines from various companies do completely different types.

The higher up the ladder you go the more choices you will have in number of buttonhole types on one machine. Sometimes, more

A trashy buttonhole ruins a garment, so choose the very best buttonhole system – GOOD but SIMPLE

than one system will produce the buttonholes e.g. memorised or sensor. The price of the machine, though, does not necessarily decree the perfection or simplicity of producing a buttonhole: there are some very modest machines on the market that will do an excellent buttonhole, performed to a professional finish – but you may only get one shape and system on a lower priced machine.

Over the years I have used the various types of automatic buttonholes extensively and can recommend all of them as being proficient and easy to perform . . .

If you are buying a machine, try the buttonholes out in the shop. If this feature is particularly important to you try all the various systems available on your chosen model for although the various systems work well YOU will probably prefer one above the rest – go with what you personally find easiest.

The Choices Of Buttonholes

The traditional square ended buttonhole will be on all machines and the key-hole is now on very many. A lot of machines will also have one square end and one round end; two round ends; a key-hole with a pointed end; a stretch buttonhole which usually has criss-cross

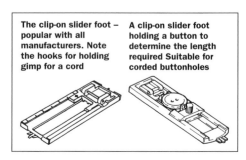

The clip-on slider foot – popular with all manufacturers. Note the hooks for holding gimp for a cord

A clip-on slider foot holding a button to determine the length required Suitable for corded buttonholes

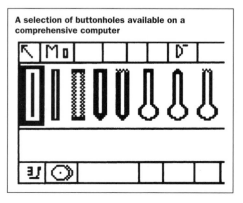

A selection of buttonholes available on a comprehensive computer

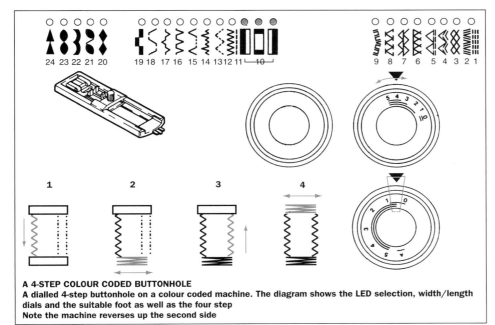

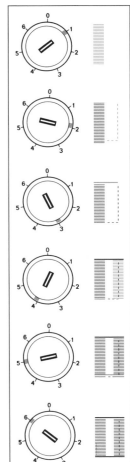

A 4-STEP COLOUR CODED BUTTONHOLE
A dialled 4-step buttonhole on a colour coded machine. The diagram shows the LED selection, width/length dials and the suitable foot as well as the four step
Note the machine reverses up the second side

5-STEP MECHANICAL BUTTONHOLE
A dialled 5-step buttonhole + securing stitching at no. 6. Note that at step 2. the machine returns to the top of the buttonhole with straight stitches so that the second side of the buttonhole is stitched with forward satin stitch

(cross-stitch-type) stitching rather than satin stitch: most top computers will do automatic eyelets too.

In the medium price range you can easily get two or three of the buttonholes listed – at the top of the range you would expect to get them all.

Popular 'Automatic' Buttonhole Systems

The 4/5-step 'dialled' buttonhole
The most basic automatic buttonhole is usually dialled in 4/5 steps: by turning a stitch selector at each stage the machine will self adjust and do bar tack, 1st side, bar tack, 2nd side. Some models will insert an extra step and do a row of straight stitches back to the beginning on step 4 so that step 5 is stitched forwards to match step 1. You decide on the length and alter the 'dial' at the marked length, before you begin you adjust the stitch length to a satin stitch. Often the slider foot is supplied to grip the fabric well.

This is dramatically better than the 'turn-around' method described earlier.

The 1-step buttonhole
With this very simple system the button tucks into the back (or front!) of the special buttonhole presser foot and having selected 'buttonhole' the machine will stitch the whole sequence the required size. This is a popular and very successful method of deciding the length and used even on many top models because it works so well – the method of

A 1-STEP BUTTONHOLE
The one-step buttonhole where the length is determined by the button in the foot PLUS the 'Push' lever can be found on mechanical and computer models.
Various types of buttonholes (square, round, keyhole etc.) are possible with this type of foot including corded ones.
Depending on the model, the route will either be as shown 1,2,3,4 (above) or with more advanced models they will take the route of the 5-step version (shown above) so that both rows of satin stitches are stitched in the same direction.
Note, whatever route the machine takes after depressing the foot control to start, the machine will complete the buttonhole in ONE operation without touching the controls – to start the next buttonhole, the 'push' lever is pushed backwards and a matching buttonhole will be performed.

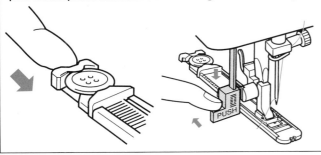

buttonholes

35

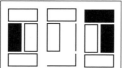

selection will, of course, differ. The 'push' lever illustrated, is to enable the machine to repeat the operation. This seems a fool-proof system.

Memorised buttonholes

- 'Memorised' buttonholes are usually selected rather like the 'dialled' version – however, once the first one is stitched the machine will memorise it and then complete the circuit, stop and lock off, each time you want to repeat it.
  This is simple and effective but sometimes you can go further and put that buttonhole into a 'memory bank' to return to it time and time again in the future. These work well.

- 'Memorised' buttonholes can come in a slightly different form however. You will find some models where the buttonhole alternative sizes are already programmed by the manufacturer: when you want to stitch a buttonhole you merely tell the machine which size you want and it stitches it out for you without any fuss! These are usually very efficient but the length is calculated in metric rather than imperial.

Sensor buttonholes

'Sensor' buttonholes are a mixture of 'memorised' and the 'button in the foot' method depending on what make or model you have. The foot incorporates within it a sensor which picks up signals from the electronics in the head of the machine during stitching: the button is placed in the foot to regulate the size. The required shape of 'buttonhole' is obtained via the stitch selector i.e. square end, round, key-hole. Again, this seems a fool-proof system.

- Machines with memorised buttonholes can sometimes provide alternative feet for buttonholing.

- The slider foot seems more or less standard these days. This usually has rubber strips underneath to hold the fabric securely during stitching.

- A clear plastic foot – of normal size – is sometimes provided as well.
  This plastic foot means that you can clearly see through to any markings which is most helpful when determining the length of the first buttonhole. There is no doubt that on occasions a small foot such as this is a boon for getting into difficult places where some of the extremely enormous button/sliders are just too bulky.

- These smaller feet always have a point in common – a grove or grooves underneath to allow the buttonhole to sit squarely under the foot with adequate clearance for a successful satin stitch and the foot holding the fabric firmly around the out side.

You can also use these feet for satin stitch embroidery!

Corded Buttonholes

Whilst hand stitchers may cord a buttonhole it is unusual for a machine sewer to do so despite the fact that most buttonhole feet allow for it.
The buttonhole is stronger and neater and simple to perform so once you have tried it you will surely go back to this method repeatedly.

- The diagram shows clearly where the cord lies during stitching. There is a hook at the back of the foot to hold the cord in place and it tucks easily into the grooves underneath. Some feet have a fork on the front to hold the loose ends, some do not . . . you just hold them during stitching.
  Select and stitch the buttonhole in the usual way: after stitching you will be able to pull one side so that the 'loop' slides down and disappears into the bar-tack.
  The ends can be snipped off, or with a needle, taken through the other side and darned in – a matter of choice depending on what you are making.

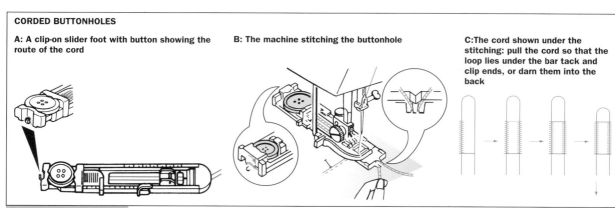

CORDED BUTTONHOLES

A: A clip-on slider foot with button showing the route of the cord

B: The machine stitching the buttonhole

C: The cord shown under the stitching: pull the cord so that the loop lies under the bar tack and clip ends, or darn them into the back

The cord used in hand stitched button holes was traditionally tailors gimp which although hard to get around the shops is still made and sold by Empress Mills. Cords suitable for machine stitched buttonholes can include crochet cotton, buttonhole twist and even two/three strands of ordinary sewing thread laid together. All will work well: decide on the suitable cord in relation to the fabric. I would recommend that the colour of the cord matches the thread, but if you cannot get an exact match, then match the cord to the fabric.

The resulting buttonhole is a little raised up, feels firmer and it certainly makes the buttonhole wear better.

The loop of the cord should be at the end where the button sits when the garment is buttoned up!

Cutting The Buttonhole

Most people slit the buttonhole with the buttonhole cutter that is usually provided with the machine. (It came to be used as a 'stitch ripper' later on!) Place a pin across the ends to stop nicking the bar-tack by mistake!

If you prefer to use scissors then they must be exceedingly sharp and pointed.

I recommend a buttonhole chisel and once you have used this method you will never go back to an alternative. The chisel is exactly that, it looks like a mini carpenters chisel, and so extremely sharp that they usually come with a little 'hat' on the offending end. A small block of wood is placed under the buttonhole, the chisel slices easily and oh! so neatly, through the fabric.

Hey presto . . . a buttonhole that is so neat it is barely visible that it has been cut at all!

CHECK LIST

Always try them out in the shop before purchase.

Always use an interfacing! (even if the pattern does not allow for it).

Always use a white interfacing in a light coloured fabric and charcoal/back interfacing in a dark coloured fabric.

Always, always, always, do test buttonholes on off-cuts of fabric to make sure you have the correct size!

Always do the test buttonhole on the same mix. of fabric and interfacing, and on the same grain lines.

Always do the buttonhole in the most difficult position last – start with those easiest to get to . . . and on the front of a garment work UP from the bottom one so that the one at the neckline (eye-line to those observing you!) benefits from the 'practice' of the others!

Always cut AFTER stitching – preferably with a chisel.

Fine-tune your satin stitches, but if they are too close the buttonhole will be stiff and unsightly.

Try cording for the best looking buttonhole and one that will be strongest in wear.

NEVER, NEVER try to do a machine buttonhole with buttonhole twist – it is far too thick . . . save the twist to use as a cord.

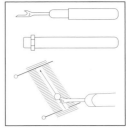

To cut open the buttonholes with the cutter supplied with the machine, place a pin across each end INSIDE the bar tack and slice from the centre to the ends

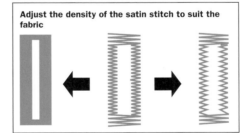

Adjust the density of the satin stitch to suit the fabric

REINFORCED BUTTONHOLES
Some models doing a 1-step buttonhole will sew the satin stitch over a straight line of stitches on both sides whatever shape is chosen

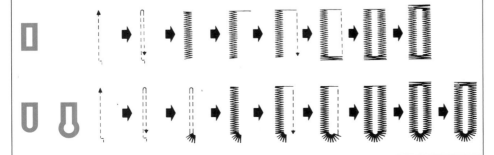

buttonholes

techniques and presser feet

A technique is a specialist operation that you require the machine to perform, such as a buttonhole, zipper insertion and quilting.

In fact, most 'stitches' can be performed with the basic sewing foot – but there are many times that it helps to use the special foot for the job in hand.

It may be as simple as a clear foot to see through to your top stitching . . . it may be as involved as a ruffler for yards and yards of frills . . . but whichever it is, choose it and use it to get the best from your machine.

Techniques usually require a particular stitch to perform the operation, and they also usually need a specialist presser foot: when feet clip on and off easily, this is not a chore.

If a specialist foot is provided it really is advisable to use it for best results. A lot of time and effort has been taken by manufacturers designing and developing these aids to perfect stitch craft.

The recommended foot for the technique will be listed in the manufacturer's handbook and they are usually numbered or lettered for identification. In some cases this data can be indicated on the machine itself when the required stitch is programmed, clearly visible, for instance on an LCD readout panel or LCD sensor panel. This chapter covers the main techniques available on a wide variety of machines.

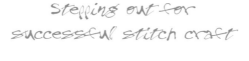

Stepping out for successful stitch craft

Feet That Come With The Machine

The set of feet illustrated is an average assortment of those you might expect to find in a mid-range machine and we will use them as an example of a reasonable selection.

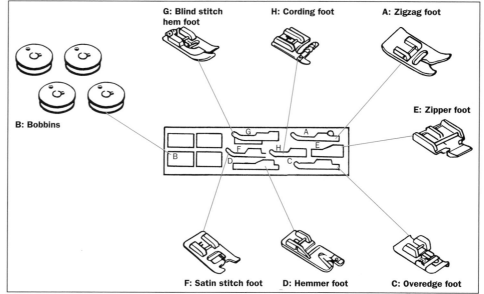

A selection of presser feet supplied with a mid-range machine. They are all labelled and stowed away for easy access/safety in a fitted tray: the bigger buttonhole foot will be in the accessory box with screwdriver etc.

G: Blind stitch hem foot
H: Cording foot
A: Zigzag foot
E: Zipper foot
B: Bobbins
F: Satin stitch foot
D: Hemmer foot
C: Overedge foot

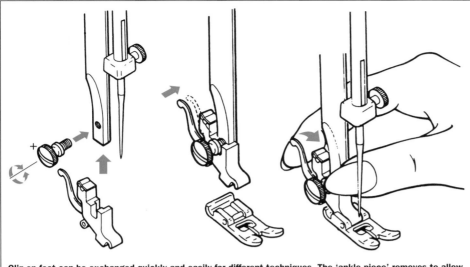

Straight stitch foot without a wide slit

Clip-on zig-zag foot

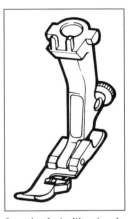

Overedge foot with extra pin to stitch over

Clip-on rolled hem foot

Clip-on feet can be exchanged quickly and easily for different techniques. The 'ankle piece' removes to allow for specialist feet to be screwed on instead.

■ With the most basic model you may just get a zig-zag foot, zipper foot and button hole foot and with a top of the range machine you could get walking feet and all manner of extras!

■ It is a fact that Bernina provide – with the machine – the largest range of feet but many other manufacturers make sure you are well catered for by providing feet for the most usual tasks and remember, you can always purchase the very specialist ones at a later date if you do, in fact, require them.

■ Remember, most machines now on the market will have clip-on feet . . . and when you need to screw on a specialist foot you should unscrew the whole ankle piece.

Straight/zig-zag

Most machines will come with a dual purpose foot but it is possible to get a straight stitch foot with a small round central hole. The width of the slit in the foot to facilitate the swing of the needle will depend on the maximum stitch width available: it used to be 5mm but machines now go to 7mm/9mm and beyond. If you buy/replace a foot, ensure that you have one wide enough for your needle swing.

Overedge

When you stitch over the edge of the fabric there is quite a pull on the sewing thread that can easily cause some puckering of the material, especially a fine or soft one. An over-edge foot will have some means of putting slightly more thread around the edge of the fabric, such as a pin that you stitch over. These feet vary from make to make but the overall job is the same.

Rolled hem

By inserting the fabric into the cork-screw shape on the front of the foot, the fabric will roll over during stitching.

Use straight stitch or zig-zag for a decorative effect.

Zipper foot

There are various types of clip-on and screw on feet available and they do tend to differ quite a lot. However, they all do the same job and will help you to stitch right on the outside edge of the foot, to ensure you are pressed well against the zip teeth, piping cord (or other 'hard' item in craft work such as a cardboard 'inner').

Craft foot

These can vary too, sometimes metal, sometimes plastic and with various shapes cut away, marks for aligning stitching and so on.

■ The satin stitch foot will be similar.

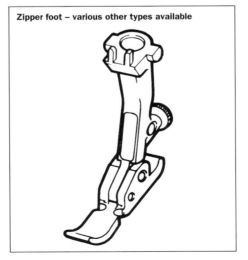

Zipper foot – various other types available

BLIND HEM FEET

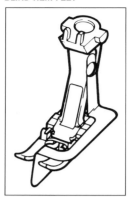

Bernina with built-in guide

Clip-on with adjustable guide

Cording foot for 3 cords

SATIN STITCH FEET

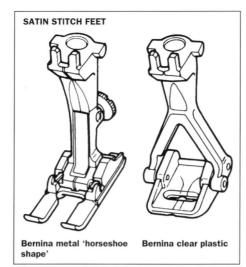

Bernina metal 'horseshoe shape'   **Bernina clear plastic**

Satin stitch foot/embroidery foot

These feet are usually clear plastic and some-times double as a small buttonhole foot but metal ones are available.

- If the foot is metal – like the Bernina foot – it may be cut away into a 'horseshoe' shape.

- The plastic feet have two main plus points: you can easily see what you are stitching and there is a groove underneath that your satin stitch (or buttonhole) will easily glide through. A clear plastic one may be cut away, but it will certainly be easy to see through the plastic.

- Use them for all the jobs where you need clear vision to the stitches underneath and position of your design, top stitching etc.

Blind hem

Blind hems are straightforward to stitch, it is the folding of the fabric that causes problems! It is vital to fold the fabric back-on-itself so that the stitching is done on the HEM allowance and the side-ways stitch takes the tiniest piece of the main fabric of the skirt, curtain etc.

- To make this calculation easier, the blind hem foot contains a movable gauge to set against the fold of the fabric. These are simpler to use than the 'blind hem gauge' which was a black metal insert of strange shape previously supplied to be used with the zig-zag foot.

Cording foot

The foot illustrated is for 'couching down' cords from above. One or more fine cords – such as crochet cotton, wool etc. – can be threaded through the grooves and then zig-zag or an embroidery stitch used to hold them down for decorative effect.

- Do not confuse these with the grooved feet which can be used for 'cording' which are mentioned later.

Buttonhole foot

These vary enormously from tiny little clear feet, through to slider feet and into the larger sensor feet.

There are also the feet which measure with a roller and all sorts of other 'aids' to help with the buttonhole. Rest assured, that the one that comes with your machine will be up to the job and will have been specially select-ed for the TYPE of buttonhole(s) your machine performs.

- Look for those that have 'hooks' so that you can easily do a corded buttonhole. If you have a very basic machine a 'corded buttonhole foot' may not be included, but can be purchased separately as they are easily obtained.

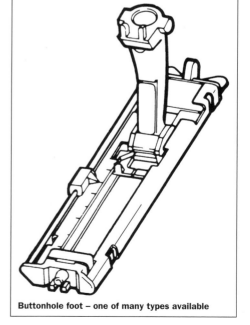

Buttonhole foot – one of many types available

Quilting guide

Now that feet clip-on there is often a small hole in the 'ankle' piece that will hold the guide . . . some machines, though, still have guides that fit onto the zip foot. No matter how they fit on they all work the same way . . . adjust the curve of the guide the distance from the needle that you want your stitching lines to be apart. Stitch the first line, and then placing the guide on the line just sewn, stitch the next, and so on until you have completed your job. You can also use the guide for accurate edging, top stitching, braid placement etc. by adjusting the guide in a similar way.

Extra Presser Feet . . . For Unusual Or Specialist Purposes

There are many feet available that will probably not be supplied with the machine.

There are just too many to illustrate each and every one! However, all the companies have a similar list and if your dealer is unhelpful contact the manufacturers head office for information.

Those illustrated are mainly Bernina feet

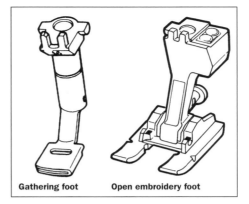

Gathering foot   **Open embroidery foot**

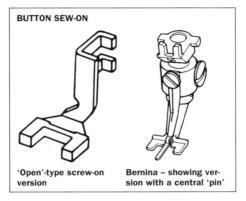

BUTTON SEW-ON

'Open'-type screw-on version   **Bernina – showing version with a central 'pin'**

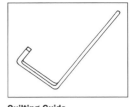

Quilting Guide

TAILOR TACK/FRINGING FEET

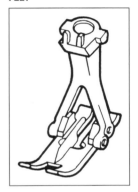

Bernina

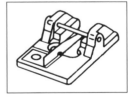

Clip-on

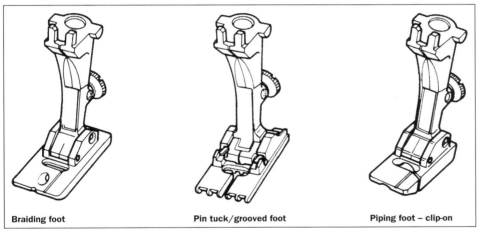

Braiding foot   **Pin tuck/grooved foot**   **Piping foot – clip-on**

Jeans foot

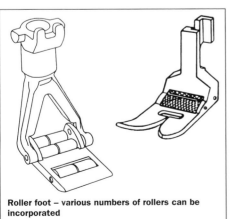

Roller foot – various numbers of rollers can be incorporated

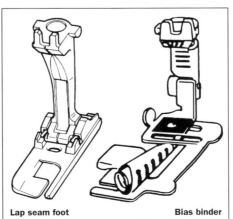

Lap seam foot   **Bias binder**

WALKING FOOT

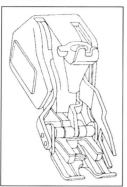

Bernina fitting

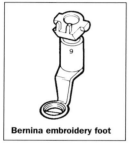

Bernina embroidery foot

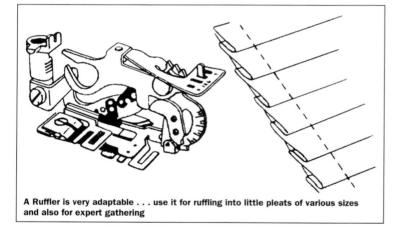

A Ruffler is very adaptable . . . use it for ruffling into little pleats of various sizes and also for expert gathering

(you can tell by the top fitting) and any clip-on and screw-on versions are from Brother or Janome but others are available.

Remember too, that feet can be 'cross pollinated' from make to make (except Bernina) if you check the shank length.

Techniques Made Easier By Using Specialist Presser Feet

Appliqué

Appliqué is extensively used in fashion/dress, craft work, household items, children's clothes and toy making. The term indicates the application by stitching of one fabric on to another in a (usually) decorative manner.

◾ Lay the motif or design on to the base fabric, tack or pin and then stitch around the design with a decorative stitch. Satin stitch can be used, as can blanket or other craft stitch.

◾ Use the embroidery/clear plastic foot supplied to see the fabric edge clearly whilst sewing.

Basting

Basting is the American term for tacking and it is now the accepted universal term for machine tacking. There are various methods.

◾ Some computer models have a stitch programme, which means you just make your selection and the machine automatically produces the long tacking stitch and the basic/normal zig-zag sewing foot is used. (Bernina, Elna, Singer).

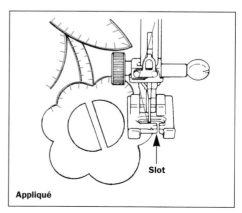

Slot

Appliqué

Another method is to select 'basting' plus the straight stitch, and drop the feed dog; the machine will produce one stitch and stop. The operator pulls the fabric to the required position of the next stitch, depresses the pedal again and one more stitch is made. Work down the length to be tacked. The stitch can be as long or short as required.

One machine uses a special short basting needle (Necchi).

Blind hem

Blind hemming is designed for turning up hems on trousers, skirts, and curtains to give a secure finish. It should be noted that this is not an INVISIBLE hem which sewers often expect it to be!

On thick tweedy or 'bulked' fabrics the stitches are less likely to show than the hem done on fine fabrics, where a small stitch is normally visible on the right side.

Do not use on a very full skirt or bias cut garment.

Use the blind hem foot supplied and follow the instructions in the illustration.

Cording

The cording foot will hold up to three or more fine cords or threads. Because they are attached to the foot, the required design can be easily followed and the cords are perfectly placed to be couched down into the desired position on the material. A variety of utility, craft or embroidery stitches can be sewn over the cords as a couching stitch. The basic design, the cord and the couching stitch and thread all contribute to the final effect.

Darning

Forwards and backwards stitching with tricot stitch adjusted to a short stitch length provides a firm darn on most fabrics. This can be sewn with the basic zig-zag foot.

By attaching the embroidery/darning foot ('hopping foot') and dropping the feed dog the traditional machine darn is achieved by random stitching over the torn area.

Specialist pre-programmed darn sequences are a feature of computer machines.
In all instances, 'darn' is selected and the machine will perform the stitch sequence and stop. If the area to be mended is large, move the fabric and repeat the darn sequence until the area is covered.

For added strength with all darning, it is recommended that a piece of lining or interfacing is placed behind the torn area.

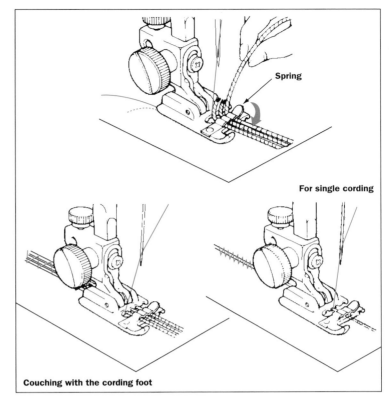

For single cording

Couching with the cording foot

Elastic stitching

A number of stitches are available for stitching on elastic and experimentation will show the best ones to the various applications. Ladder stitch, for example, will stitch to either side of a knicker-type elastic whilst encasing it in under a row of stitches across the top. Tricot zig-zag is stitched directly through the taught elastic and the fabric has a pretty crimped effect when the elastic springs back into place.

The zig-zag foot can be used but one with a wide groove underneath to sit astride the elastic will make the job easier.

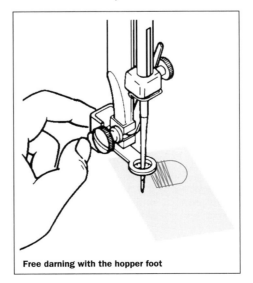

Free darning with the hopper foot

DARNING

A simple darn with tricot stitch

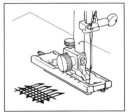

Pre-programmed darning sequence

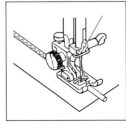

Encasing a cord elastic with zig-zag using the grooved foot

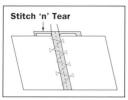

Stitch 'n' Tear

Faggotting

Elastic strip is available in various widths. One or more rows of elastic can be used for ankles, cuffs, bodices and so on.
The elastic is pulled out tight then machine stitch rows of straight stitch between the elastic cords (and over the netting in between). When completed, the effect is the same as rows of shirring – but this technique is considerably easier! A grooved foot is the ideal one to use.

For swimwear, choose elastic that is specifically recommended. The best for the job is cotton braid swimwear elastic. This comes in a variety of widths and is usually sold by the yard off large spools. It is very durable; it retains its stretch ability when stitched through and its shape when wet. Other elastics suitable for swimwear are polyester knit elastic. Avoid acetate elastic for swimwear; it loses its shape when wet, which means you may lose your suit!

Be sure to use the correct width of elastic as called for in the pattern instructions. Each width of elastic has a different amount of stretch and is not interchangeable without altering the fit of your suit.

Faggotting
Faggotting is the joining of two pieces or strips of fabric with decorative stitching, but leaving a gap between the fabrics.

Traditionally the pieces were laid onto paper, but Vilene Stitch 'n' Tear should be substituted for the paper as this works very well and it is more easily removed.

The method is to turn under the seam allowance and lay the pieces to be joined onto the Stitch 'n' Tear, butting them together and then tack or pin, so that during the stitching the S 'n' T holds the fabrics evenly spaced. When the S 'n' T is torn away, the seam will have a decorative 'spaced' effect.

Use Feather stitch, Vine stitch or a similar embroidery stitch.

Use the normal zig-zag presser foot. Some machines provide a guide to keep the fabrics evenly spaced.

Gathering
Do not confuse gathering with ruffling . . .
Simple gathers are done with the basic foot and a long straight stitch. Do a trial BEFORE considering loosening the tension, which often is not required with this method.

Sew TWO rows about 6mm (¼") apart and then pull up both rows together with the BOBBIN (underneath) thread.

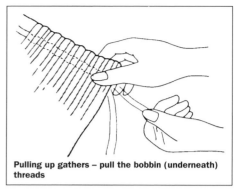

Pulling up gathers – pull the bobbin (underneath) threads

Some machines have a gathering foot supplied but it is usually an 'extra' purchase. This foot merely ensures a slackening of tension or a looser stitch.

Overlocking
This term, often used for all the 'seam and overcast' stitches, is usually used wrongly. "Overlock" is a patented trade name and it applies to an 'overlocking machine' not to the 'copy' performed by a domestic machine. Using the terminology 'over-edging' or 'neatening' is more factually correct. Whatever the instruction book calls it, no normal domestic machine will do a true overlock stitch apart from the Janome 'Combi' machine.

Various presser feet are supplied for this neatening function and/or the seam and overcast in one operation. Most incorporate a small wire prong; sometimes there are two or three prongs. When the stitch is sewn, the action of the needle passing the thread over the prongs will put extra thread into the stitch sequences so that the edges are less likely to buckle or pucker. This foot is used when the threads actually bind or oversew the cut edge.

Some seam and over-edge stitches – such as the knit stitch – sew not over the edge but up to it. The pronged foot would not be used in this instance as the stitch formation is different. Either an alternative overlocking foot is provided, or the normal presser foot can be used.

Various factors contribute to the finish obtained: fabric in use, thread, needle, type of stitch, type of machine and so on. No hard and fast rules can be given. However, if excessive puckering occurs, **DECREASE THE STITCH WIDTH** do not adjust the tension as a first move. An alternative is not to sew over the edge but to sew inside the edge of the seam allowance, that is to put the edge of the foot on the edge of the fabric and then trim after stitching.

Opinions differ as to whether to trim the 16mm (⅝") seam allowance in dressmaking

Samples of 'overlocking'/over-edging using the over-edge foot

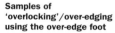

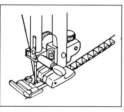

Knit stitch sewn on the seam line and trimmed afterwards using the zig-zag foot

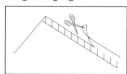

before or after stitching. Again, there are no hard and fast rules as it depends on the stitch in use and the fabric. A test piece is required to decide which stitch is best suited to the job in hand, and this will determine whether the seam allowance is cut/trimmed before or after stitching.

Piping
Piping is the insertion of a thick cord into a bias cut strip of fabric. This is then inserted into a seam line for decorative purposes on dress, upholstery and various craft items.

▪ Use the zipper foot to make the piping strip and for insertion into the seam.

▪ Alternatively, piping feet that have a tunnel to encase the cord during stitching are now available for many different makes.

Quilting
Quilted fabric is two or three layers sewn together, one of which is a wadding/bulked fabric. It is usual to have the top fabric, then the wadding, and then either lining or interfacing on the bottom. Butter muslin is ideal as a backing/interfacing for this job on most fabrics. The fabrics must be well anchored together with tacking stitches. It is best to start stitching from the centre of the fabric and work out to each side. Mark the first stitching line, then stitch; move the fabric across and place the quilting guide on the stitching line, then sew; move as before.

▪ Quilting is most effective with decorative stitches rather than just the straight stitch, particularly on plain fabrics. It is simple to do but it does take a lot of thread, so remember to purchase extra reels.

▪ Quilting is traditionally done in diamond shapes, but with modern interpretation it can be in squares, tramlines and other geometric styles.

▪ Using the darning/embroidery foot, it is possible to follow a design or pattern freely whilst quilting.

Rolled hem
Even the most basic zig-zag machine will usually come supplied with a rolled hem foot.

Not a favourite – this has to be the foot that causes most problems and if you have an overlocker, abandon your rolled hems to that!

▪ If you are determined to use this foot, the advice is . . . use a very fine cloth, and slice the corner off before you start. Roll the beginning of the edge and push it into the 'screw-type area' at the front of the foot. Make sure you reach the needle, drop the needle and the foot, hold the threads out BEHIND the foot and 'help' the fabric through as you begin to stitch. As you stitch, 'roll' the fabric 'into' the 'screw-area' by pulling the fabric to the left. Try and keep it rolled as you help it through!

Shell tucks and shell edging
This is an alternative edging for lingerie, babywear, and so on, and for use as a decorative finish. The fabric should be fine, such as crepe de Chine or tricot. Use the blind hem stitch and tighten the top tension to pull the

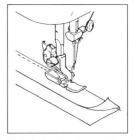

Piping with the zipper foot

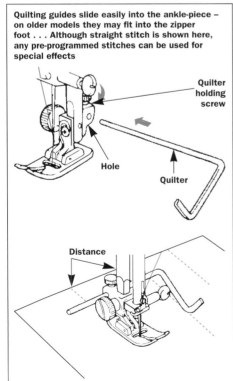

Quilting guides slide easily into the ankle-piece – on older models they may fit into the zipper foot . . . Although straight stitch is shown here, any pre-programmed stitches can be used for special effects

Quilter holding screw

Hole

Quilter

Distance

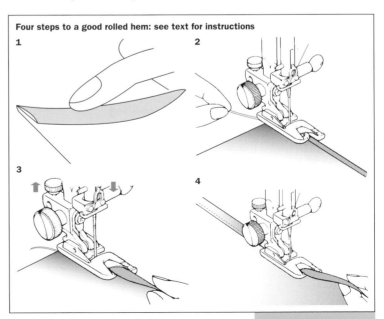

Four steps to a good rolled hem: see text for instructions

1

2

3

4

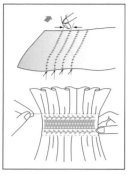

Machine Smocking can be fun, quick, and very effective

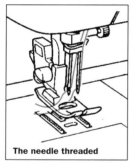

Shell tucking & Shell edging are simple to stitch and very pretty

side-stitch in towards the other stitches, thus causing a 'pucker' that has a shell/scallop shape. Shell tucks are best sewn on the bias.

▦ Use the zig-zag foot or clear plastic foot.

Smocking

Smocking on the sewing machine is most effective, creative and simple. However, do not expect the exact, regimented stitches of the hand embroideress.

▦ The area to be smocked must be gathered by rows of stitching in the usual way. Stroke the gathers with a pin to ensure that they lie smoothly. A test piece will ascertain which of your stitches are most effective; satin and open embroidery stitches are suitable used on a variety of stitch widths.

▦ Use the clear embroidery foot.

Twin needle sewing

Most automatic machines take a twin needle. This is two needles on one shank, which is inserted into the machine in the normal manner.

▦ Thread the machine with two reels of thread of matching or contrast colours. There is still only one bobbin thread, and it can be a good idea to match this thread to the fabric if two contrasting top threads are being used.

▦ Use the normal presser foot except when tucking.

▦ The twin needle control should be used if there is one on the machine. This reduces the needle swing to ensure that the second needle does not hit the presser foot. If you do not have such a control, great care should be taken to keep the needle swing within the width of the presser foot.

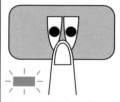

The needle threaded

An example of a twin needle control button Note: more about Twin Needle sewing in the chapter on Needles

Twin needle pin tucks

Twin needle top stitching
Two identical rows of top stitching are possible for jeans and fashion garments.

Twin needle embroidery stitching
Embroidery stitches of all kinds can be used for a variety of decorative effects.

Twin needle tucking
If the bottom (bobbin) tension is tightened considerably, a tucked effect will be obtained. This is particularly nice on jersey fabrics or soft cottons or lawn.

Use a grooved foot if tucks are very close together.

Twin needle tucking with insertion cord
The tucks are obtained in the same way as for twin needle tucking. Before stitching, insert a cord through the needle plate of the machine. As the machine stitches, the cord is automatically fed into the back of the tuck. This provides an extremely attractive finish with a pronounced ridged effect.

▦ Machines without the hole in the needle plate often provide an alternative method to hold the cord – see your manufacturer's handbook.

Twin needle decorative hem stitching
Decorative hem stitching is enhanced by using the twin-wing needle. Use this needle in the normal twin-stitching way and select the required stitch. Many models have special hem stitches. Hem stitching is a craft technique and should not be confused with turning hems on garments.

Zippers . . .
Zipper feet vary enormously from make to make, in size and shape.

▦ Screw-on zipper feet have a slider incorporated so that the foot can be easily placed to either side of the needle, whichever side is the most convenient during stitching.

▦ It is now more usual to have a clip-on zipper foot because the needle position can be moved easily to the correct point for stitching. The foot can clip on in left, right or centre positions too. Zipper feet, therefore, are much smaller and neater than their predecessors. Although they do vary in basic shape somewhat, most do a very successful job.

▦ Invisible zipper feet are not often supplied with the machine although a few companies do provide a clip-on invisible zipper foot as an extra purchase. A screw-on version is available to fit many makes and models of machine.

. . . Concealed zipper insertion

This is the traditional way to insert a zip into a skirt or trousers with a side opening or with a fly front.

■ To prepare the fabric, place the right sides together and sew to the end of the zipper opening. Reverse stitch to knot the stitches. Sew the zipper opening with basting stitches.

■ To insert the zip, fold back the left seam allowance. Turn under the right seam allowance to form a 0.2 to 0.3cm (⅛") fold. Place the zipper teeth next to the fold and pin in place.

■ Lower the needle into the fabric at the point where sewing is to begin, then lower the foot. Sew through fold and zipper tape. Stop just before the zipper foot reaches the slider on the zipper tape. Turn the balance wheel by hand and lower the needle into the fabric. Raise the zipper foot and open the zipper. Lower the foot and stitch the remainder of the seam.

■ Close the zipper and spread the fabric flat with the right side facing up. Move the zipper foot to the left pin. Guide the edge of the foot along the zipper teeth and stitch through garment and zipper tape. Stop about 5cm (2") from the top of the zipper. With the needle down in the fabric, raise the foot, remove the basting stitches and open the zipper. Then lower the foot and stitch the remainder of the seam, making sure the fold is even.

. . . Semi-concealed zipper insertion

For a long back zip or a centre front opening on a dress or tunic, the concealed zip opening will give the same amount of overlap each side of the teeth.

■ To prepare the fabric, place the right sides of the fabric together and sew to the end of the zipper opening. Reverse stitch to knot the stitches.

■ Sew the zipper opening with basting stitches. Open out and press.

■ Insert the zip as follows. With zipper foot against the teeth of the zip, stitch down, across and up the other side. Take great care when stitching across the zipper not to break the needle. Nylon and polyester zips will sew easily here, but metal zippers can prove a problem.

. . . Fly front zipper

Iron the fly edge. Baste the closed zipper underneath the pressed right hand fly edge so that its teeth are still visible.

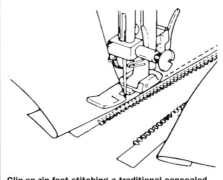

Clip-on zip foot stitching a traditional concealed zipper opening

Clip-on invisible zip foot: Pfaff

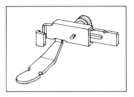

Screw-on zip foot

■ Pin the facing strip to the underside and stitch it down at the same time as you sew on the zipper. The zipper teeth move along the right hand guide edge. Shortly before you reach the end of the seam, leave the needle down in the material, raise the sewing foot and open the zipper. Then lower the foot again and sew the seam to the end.

■ Close the zipper. Fold the right edge over the left and pin it in place according to the seam line. Then baste in the left zip per chain.

■ Open the zipper. Attach the edge guide and adjust it so that its finger moves along the fabric edge. Shortly before you reach the end of the seam, leave the needle down in the material, raise the sewing foot and close the zipper. Then lower the foot again and sew to the end of the seam. Secure the end of the zipper seam with a tack.

. . . Invisible zippers

Please note that an ordinary zipper cannot be inserted invisibly.

The invisible zipper is a specialist item. They are a little more expensive (pennies not pounds!) but really are worth the little extra for the professional finish obtained and ease of insertion. Good-quality ready-to-wear garments usually have invisible (or concealed) zippers. These are sadly neglected by the home dressmaker, which is a great pity because they ensure success every time – once you know how to use them.

Invisible zippers from YKK and Coats are now widely available from the larger department stores but not often in a prominent position! They are available in two lengths: short for skirts and trousers and long for back zips or soft furnishings. You can trim the long ones to the required size.

■ This type of zipper is suitable for all fabrics from fine silk crepe de chine and silky jerseys through to suit-weight wools and tweeds, and can be inserted into

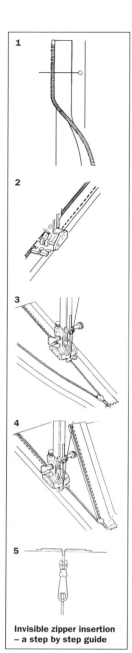

**Invisible zipper insertion
– a step by step guide**

skirts, trousers and dresses. They are totally invisible on the right side of the garment, the opening merely looks like another seam.

Use the following sequence to insert the invisible zipper and remember the zipper is laid on the RIGHT SIDE (outside) of the garment.

▪ Do not sew the seam below the zip.

▪ Open the zipper and lay the left size on the garment as illustrated – the teeth on the seam line which is usually 15mm (⅝") inside the fabric edge, and the top of the zipper opening (approximately 6mm (¼") below the waist/neck seam line). Pin into place with pins at 90 degrees to the zip. (1)

▪ With zipper foot or normal presser foot sew the zip into place on the outside edge of the tape. (2)

▪ Using the invisible zipper foot sew the stitching line under the teeth: needle in the central hole and teeth under the left-hand 'tunnel'. (3)

▪ When the foot reaches the zip pull/tag either 'lock-off' or do one or two reverse stitches to fasten off.

▪ Repeat steps 2-5 on the right-hand side of the tape and garment, using the right-hand tunnel on the foot.(4)

▪ Close zip. (5)

▪ Lay out the garment and pin or tack the seam from hemline to zipper.

▪ Stitch from the hem upwards towards the zip on the seamline, using the zipper foot with the needle on the right-hand outside of the foot: when you reach the zipper continue sewing alongside the previous stitching line for 1.25-2cm (½"-¾") and then lock-off. This overlap is vital so that there is not a 'poke' at the bottom of the zip in wear.

48

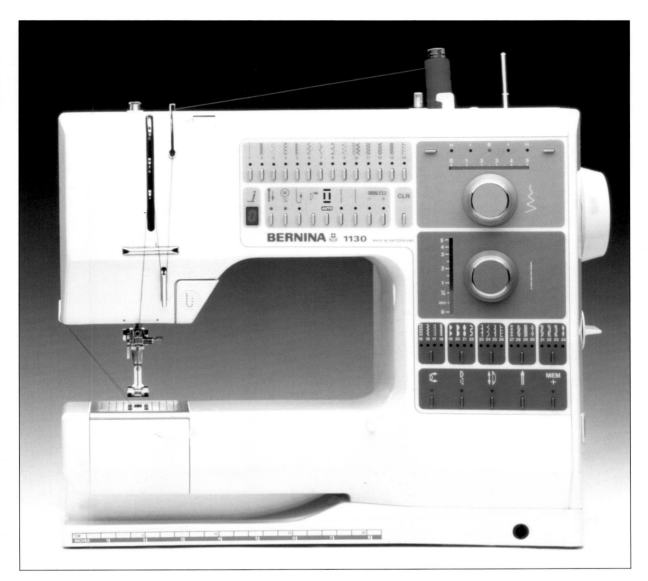

The facia of the Bernina 1130 clearly illustrates many of the points discussed on computer machines . . .

Easy thread system: Thread cutter: Free Arm: Clip-on feet: Push button stitch selection: Easy-touch dials for adjusting stitch width/length. The symbols for various techniques/stitches mentioned in their respective chapters are easily spotted: Memory, Mirror image, Elongation, Tacking, Buttonholes, Needle up/down, Needle positions, Utility stitches, Decorative stitches.

It is becoming fashionable with many manufacturers to 'hide' all this information away inside the 'plain casing' where the vast range of stitchery is activated through a liquid crystal panel instead of the push button system.

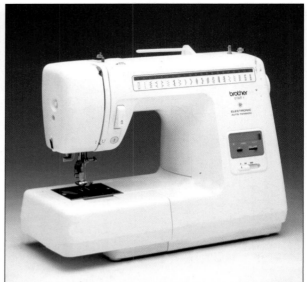

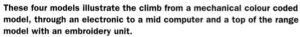

These four models illustrate the climb from a mechanical colour coded model, through an electronic to a mid computer and a top of the range model with an embroidery unit.

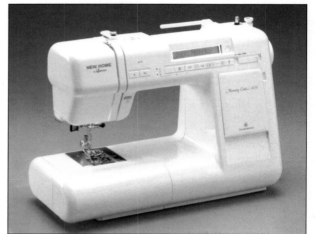

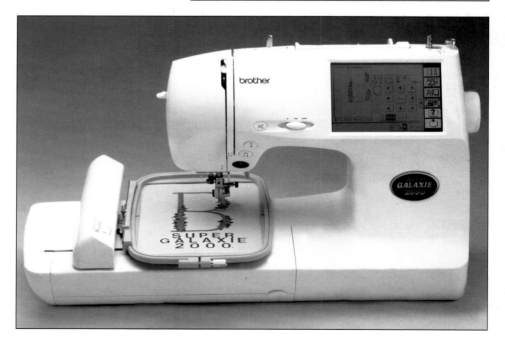

The Bernina 1630(S) is unique in using the 'mouse' for stitch selection and it can be linked to a PC for the ultimate in design creativity . . .

Above: Scanners make the copying of designs quick and efficient . . .

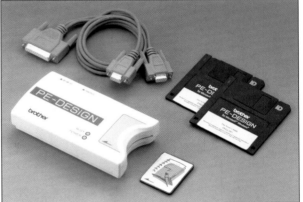

Design on a computer and transfer that design to a smart card . . .

A machine that is only capable of embroidery sewing and none of the usual 'utility' stitches in an innovative new idea.

This picture clearly shows: the drop-in bobbin with a plastic viewing cover to check how much thread remains: the screw-on ankle piece for the clip-on feet: the needle threader: the button-hole lever: the thread cutter: the reverse button & the stop/start button for use WITHOUT the foot pedal.

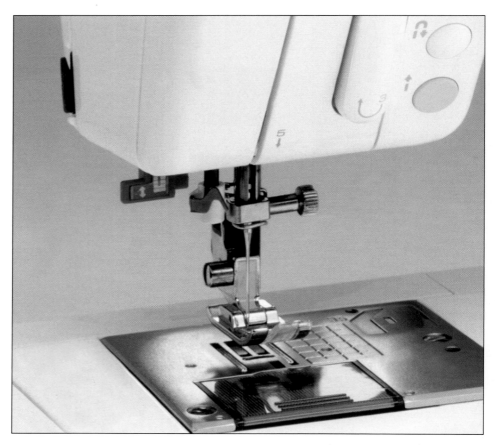

Bernina feet will always clip on higher up . . .

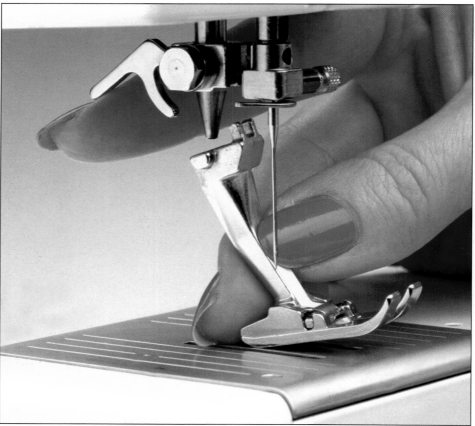

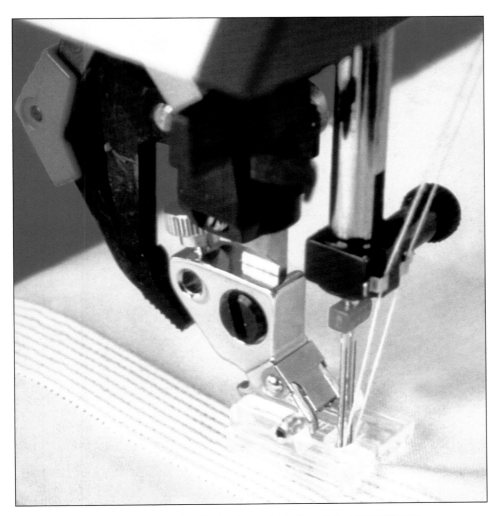

The 'wide toe' foot is excellent for embroidery or detailed stitching as the stitches are clearly visible . . .

Pfaff are the only company to have the Dual Feed system – clearly shown behind the needle area. The ankle piece has a hole/screw at the back to slot in the quilting guide, a number of other makes/models have this facility. Twin needle pin tucks can be stitched extremely close together using the grooved foot.

Stitching on 'elastic strip' using another grooved foot (clearly visible directly under the 3 in the centre hole). This type of foot can also be used for couching down decorative threads although other alternatives are available.

'Teflon' feet are designed to glide easily over problem fabrics or difficult areas of stitching – this is a clip-on version.

A screw-on 'Teflon' foot slides easily over fine, suede leather.

An example of an embroidery unit . . .

the hoop is fixed to the bar on the left which is controlled by the smart card – the hoop is thus moved from side-to-side and up-and-down during sewing to create the stitches: the needle merely pops up-and-down basically doing straight stitches. A hopper foot is necessary but not shown here.

You will note that the 'scissors' symbol is clearly shown . . . touching this button quickly snips the threads at the end of stitching.

. . . the motif is complete.

The hopper foot is clearly seen in here. The motif span is approx. 5".

When each part/colour of the design is completed, the machine will stop and wait to be re-threaded before continuing.

Small designs take up to 5 minutes whilst a very large or complicated design can take up to nearly half-an-hour to stitch out.

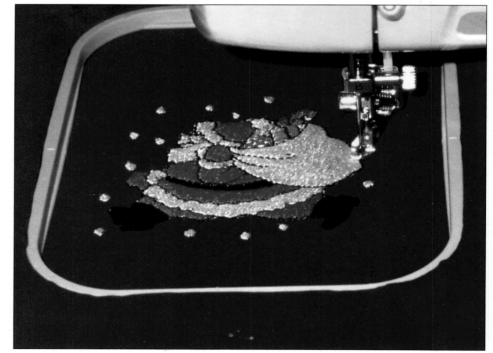

The zipper foot is traditionally used to insert piping although many companies have now developed specialist piping feet of various sizes.

Super dress bags using PVC covered cotton from Liberty of London.

The walking foot contains a feed dog – clearly seen in white each side of the needle area – which is activated by the needle bar as the foot 'walks' across the fabric.

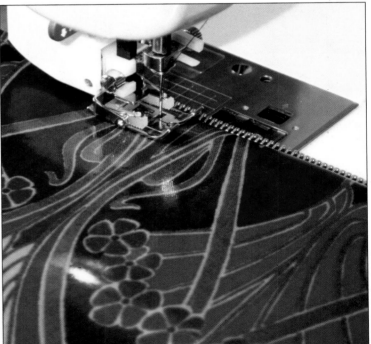

Appliqué is easier to do with a clear plastic foot: stitch first and trim afterwards.

ALWAYS INTERFACE WHERE YOU STITCH THE BUTTONHOLES!

Square ended buttonhole

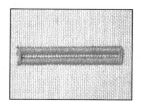

Rounded ended buttonhole

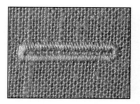

Tricot zig-zag is the perfect stitch for applying elastic.

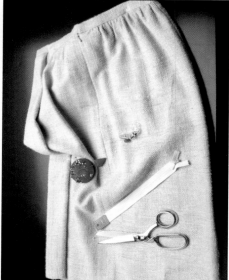

Stretch buttonhole

Interfacing not only supports the fabric during wear but supports the stitches during making up as well & top stitching will always be better where interfacing is used.

Invisible zips . . . a special foot gives a perfect finish.

Left: Built-in alphabet stitches can be used for decorative finishes, not just for name tapes.

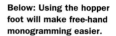

Below: Using the hopper foot will make free-hand monogramming easier.

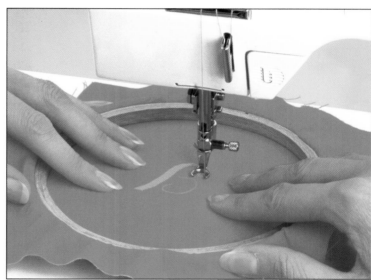

Use your needle positions to make the stitching of heading tapes easier – a Jeans needle will help with heavier upholstery fabrics.

Top stitching and edge stitching are always easier when you have a variety of needle positions. A 'saddle stitch' is being used for the top stitching/appliqué here.

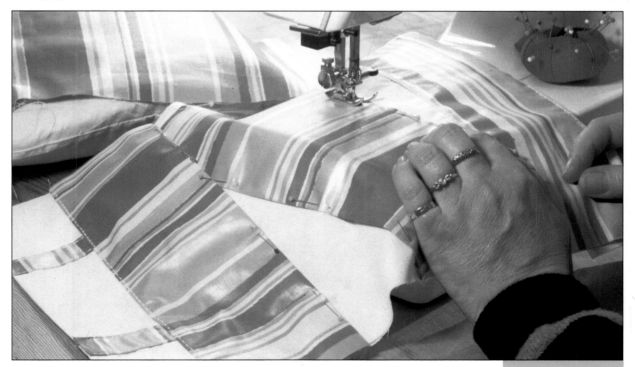

Made by Maggie Swain

The gorgeous Emeline shows off: Faggotting, twin-needle pin tucking, shell tucking, shell edging, lace appliqué & gathering.

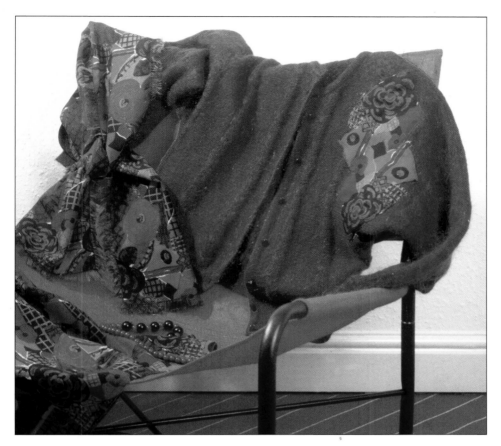

Fringing looks 'special' when edged with a tiny 'buttonhole' stitch – NOT satin stitch, but the machine equivalent of the decorative hand buttonhole stitch. The same stitch can be used for appliqué: place Stitch 'n' Tear behind the knit whilst stitching.

Twin needle pin tucks using the tricot stitch give are unusual. The tiny scallop is a decorative embroidery stitch trimmed after sewing.

Introducing texture to a picture greatly enhances the finished effect.

Using computer skills a similar design can be created to compliment the china.

Bondaweb fuses the appliqué design to the base fabric . . .

With smart card technology more complicated designs are possible . . . matching up the colours for the car & thread, the lettering & club logo – the embroidery in the hoop is supported with Stitch 'n' Tear during stitching.

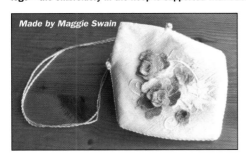

Using water soluble fabric 3-D embroidery techniques are possible.

The end product . . .

Fusible fleece can be used for warmth or quilted effects.

Using heavier threads – such as buttonhole twist –
and a decorative stitch adds texture. A bold stitch
enhances the stitches on a heavy fabric.

A huge selection of threads are available that are
suitable for machine stitching . . .

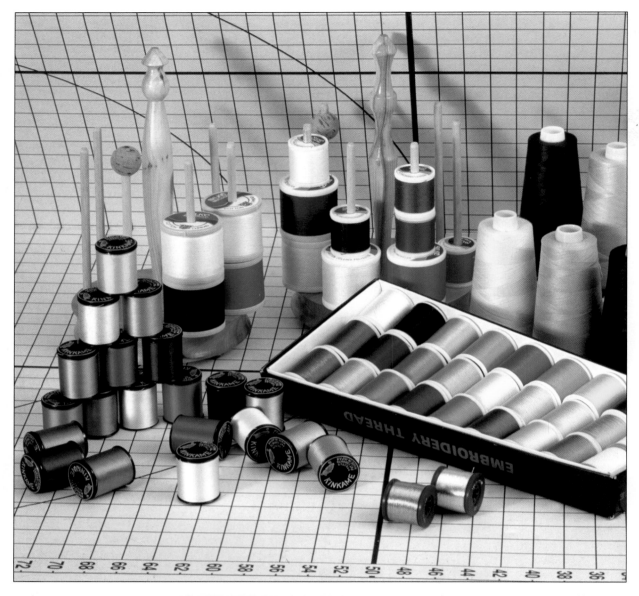

For construction, match the thread to the fabric but for embellishment, these rules can be broken!

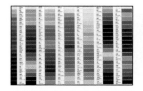

needles and threads

Needles

Some years ago manufacturers decided to make needle sizes standard for all makes of machines – this was a giant leap forward because it made it possible to use a variety of specialist needles retailed by various companies across the whole range of makes on the market.

However, if you are using an older machine take your standard needle along to the shop to make comparisons before purchase – and seek the help and advice of the specialist in the sewing machine shop or special department of the store. Although needles are available in the haberdashery areas it is the demonstrator/consultant in the sewing machine department who is trained to help and advise.

Most surprisingly, sewers often economise on needles whilst spending a lot on fabrics. However, a bad needle can ruin fabrics of all kinds and a new needle is a very minor expense for perfect stitching!

The most common 'fault' on a new machine usually turns out to be a wrongly inserted needle!

This simple rule will apply to most machines: if your bobbin goes into the machine from the side, the flat part of the needle faces the right-hand side of the machine: if the bobbin goes into the machine at the front (or behind the needle) the flat part of the needle faces away from you.

It is important to replace your needles regularly. Needles go blunt surprisingly quickly, particularly when you are using synthetic fabrics, so be prepared to change your needle after making every garment and/or sewing project. Yes! EVERY one. If your fabric contains synthetics and/or if it is a thick fabric you may need to change the needle during the project as well.

A new needle in the sewing machine is as important as a new blade in a razor – neither work well when blunt

The right size and type of needle combined with a suitable thread are two vital ingredients for successful stitching . . .

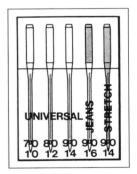

CORRECT INSERTION OF THE NEEDLE IS VITAL!
It is also desirable to tighten the needle clamp screw with a screw driver because a needle can vibrate loose during fast stitching . . .
The FLAT side of the needle faces away from you on a front or top loading machine – it faces to the right-hand side on a side-loading model.

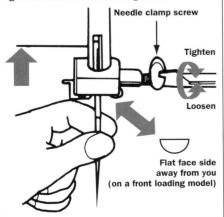

Needle clamp screw
Tighten
Loosen
Flat face side away from you (on a front loading model)

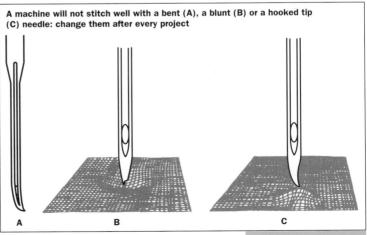

A machine will not stitch well with a bent (A), a blunt (B) or a hooked tip (C) needle: change them after every project

A   B   C

65

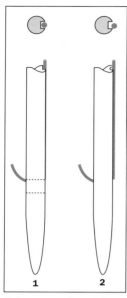

Make sure needle and thread are compatible as well as being right for the fabric being stitched.
During stitching, the thread lies in the long groove to the front of the needle (1). If the thread is too thick, or the needle too fine, the thread will not fit into the groove (2) and skipped stitches will result

NEEDLE GUIDE

Standard needle:
Normal point, slightly rounded

Special needles:
Fine ball point

Teflon-type, stretch medium point ball point

Extra fine point – size 9

Spear point

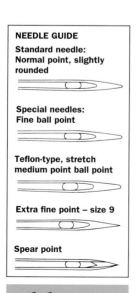

Remember too, to **THROW IT AWAY** when you have taken it out of the machine and NEVER keep it for use at a later date.

Ballpoint needles need to be changed just as often as 'sharp' ones. Blunt needles will not only damage the fibres in your fabric they will also start to skip stitches. You often skip stitches if your needle is too small or too large for the fabric you are sewing – e.g. an '18' on crêpe-de-chine or an '11' on denim.

Size '14' needles (continental size '90') were considered 'average' before synthetic and knitted fabrics made such an important impact on home sewing. A '14' is still a good choice for many medium weights of wool and cotton, but now an '11' ('70') is considered the 'average' for modern fabrics.

Numbers '16' and '18' ('100' and '120') are for coats and heavyweight sewing tasks.

Number '9' ('60') is still available from manufacturers so chivvy your local dealer if he or she does not stock them: these extra-fine needles are invaluable for excessively fine work.

A most interesting but little-known fact, is that **ballpoint needles** will work beautifully on all fabrics even 100 per cent cottons, silks and wools. Designed originally for nylons, synthetic fabrics and jersey they have now become standard for most sewing tasks. Available in packets of size '11' ('70') they can also be available in mixed-size packets occasionally.

There is an improved ballpoint called a **Scarfed needle.** Made by Janome, the difference is a technical one relating to the length of the cut-away part of the shank above the eye. Use it on all fabrics – synthetic or natural – and if not obviously available on your haberdashery shelves ask the local demonstrator/consultant. Another improved needle is the **Teflon needle.** This is black and looks just like the inside of a frying-pan. Try this for the heavier synthetic jerseys, double-knits and Crimplene-type fabrics, plushes, single knits, knits and PVC. **Jeans needles** are also a wonderful development. Extraordinarily strong, they slice through denim just like butter. Do use them, too, for upholstery work, repairs on tents, awnings, canvas sails, garden furniture and other heavyweight repair jobs.

Leather needles have a blade rather than a normal point which will slice through leather without damaging the skins. Use normal settings on your machine and a cotton or all-purpose thread for sewing seams. Embroidery on leather is perfectly practicable and in this instance the buttonhole twist can give excellent results (but use a finer thread on the bobbin). Sylko and even the pure silk threads can look marvellous on leather as well.

Most fully-automatic machines will take a **twin needle** but it seems to be the most neglected of all needles available. It is surprisingly simple and once you have sewn with it you will have many uses for the twin rows of stitches produced. It is ideal for a double top-stitching line which is always evenly spaced and for special embroidery effects. (Note: older machines or modern side-loading models will not normally take a twin needle.)

A **triple needle** can be inserted into a limited number of machines. Most of the comments on twin needles apply to triples but before purchase check that your machine will take this type of needle.

The wing needle is also very much neglected. Use for a hem-stitch finish (the wings enlarge the hole). Other stitches can have particularly good effects with this needle so experiment with your own range.

Twin needle sewing is straightforward. The needle fits into the machine like any other because it has one shank to insert into the needle clamp.

▪ Thread the machine with the two threads by placing the two 'cotton reels' onto the two thread spindles: holding both threads together go through the threading system, separating only to go through the tension discs and the thread guides above the needle, and of course the two eyes!

▪ Set the machine on straight stitch and start to sew: there will be two rows of straight lines on top of the fabric and a zig-zag underneath because, of course, there is only one bobbin thread underneath to keep the two top ones in place.

▪ Because of the width of the needle it is necessary to restrict the needle swing when doing zig-zag or embroidery stitches. On a machine with a needle swing of '5' the maximum width setting would usually be about '3', but because of the width of the needle the pattern will still be '5' when stitched. Wider swing machines will obviously have greater flexibility so refer to the handbook with your machine for guidance.

▪ To turn a corner with the twin needle: stop stitching and using the balance wheel just pierce the fabric with the left-hand needle (this is slightly longer than the right-hand one). Turn the fabric through 45 degrees. Continue sewing.

▪ It is fun to experiment with zig-zag and utility stitches and then move on to embroidery patterns to see what effects can be obtained. Two threads the same colour will give a different effect to two toning shades and a different one again will be produced by two contrasting colours, or try one metallic/lurex thread with a normal thread. Try two threads of different thickness – there are many permutations.

TWIN NEEDLE STITCHING

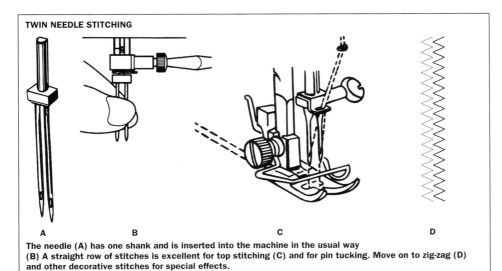

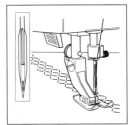

A wing needle is used for heirloom stitching and other decorative purposes

The needle (A) has one shank and is inserted into the machine in the usual way
(B) A straight row of stitches is excellent for top stitching (C) and for pin tucking. Move on to zig-zag (D) and other decorative stitches for special effects.

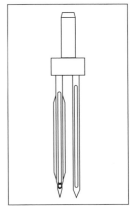

A twin wing needle – use like a normal twin: one needle will makes holes the other do normal stitching

- Some of the patterns will look better than others so it is a good idea to add samples to your 'doodle' folder with some written comments on how you achieved the desired effect.

Machine pin tucks are sewn equally easily with the twin needle.

- The machine is set up in the normal way for twin-needle sewing but the bobbin tension is increased considerably: when you stitch the bobbin thread pulls the two top threads closely together, causing a ridge in the fabric.

- A quick tip here is to do a centre row of stitches, then place the edge of the foot next to the line of stitches already sewn and sew another line. Continue in this way, moving across the piece to be tucked, always sewing in the same direction!

- Using a grooved foot will enable the pin tucks to be stitched very closely together.

- To ensure tucks further apart are evenly spaced use the quilting guide and for a more decorative pin tuck use the tricot stitch (three-step zig-zag).

- For a very pronounced tuck, or on slightly heavier fabric, insert a cord underneath the tuck.

- The tucks look most effective when left unpressed.

Threading the machine for twin needle sewing . . .
Most machines have an extra spool pin, or one can be inserted during this operation.
Hold both threads together as you go around the system: if you can see your tension discs, place one thread one side and one the other side. Separate the threads on reaching the thread guides by the needle.
To help eliminate 'twisting' of the threads during stitching, thread the right needle with the right thread and the left needle with the left thread.

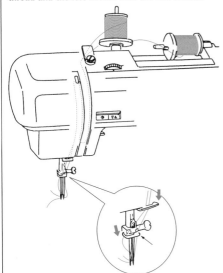

CHECK LIST

Special Check List For Needles

- Always use a NEW needle on a new project

- Insert it correctly!

- Change it regularly

- Throw it away after use!

- Ballpoint needles can be used on most fabrics

- Teflon needles are superb for quilting and also for jersey fabrics

- Bad stitching? make sure it is not blunt

- Bad stitching? make sure it is not bent

- Skipping stitches? make sure it is the right size

needles and threads

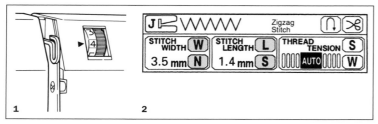

J ⊏ WWWW		Zigzag Stitch	⟲ ✂
STITCH WIDTH **W**	STITCH LENGTH **L**	THREAD TENSION **S**	
3.5 mm **N**	1.4 mm **S**	‖‖‖ AUTO ‖‖‖ **W**	

Whether tension is set by a simple manual dial (1) or state-of-the-art technology (2) . . . you need it!

ALL THREADS MUST HAVE TENSION TO FORM STITCHES CORRECTLY.

TOP THREADS must pass through the tension unit – if you miss, then you will get big loops hanging down UNDERNEATH the fabric: bobbin threads must pass through the tension spring on the bobbin holder (top load) or bobbin case (side or front load) – if they miss, then there will be big loops on the TOP of the fabric. Top thread tension can be adjusted via the dial/touch screen even when 'automatic'.

A well set up machine will rarely need the tension adjusting except for specialist operations. Check the tension by comparing top and bottom threads this is easiest with zig-zag – top and bottom should look the same. If they do not match, adjust tension as above. **DO NOT ALTER TENSION INDISCRIMINATELY!**

Bobbin tension is adjusted via the screw clearly seen in the bottom diagram which will also be present on the top loading type of bobbin holder.

Threads

There are a wide variety of threads available now for the home dressmaker and craftworker.

Most threads on cops (cotton reels) work well in the sewing machine and some have, in fact, been designed specifically for modern fabrics and machines. The majority of machines sew perfectly happily with most threads but occasionally a certain make of thread will be rejected by a machine. If your machine has been sewing perfectly well up until this particular project look to your thread before anything else. Put another make/type of thread into your machine and often it will revert to perfect stitching again.

Most people buy thread by colour: they require an excellent match between thread and fabric and so select from the various makes available within the type of thread they want to use, e.g. polyester thread, combination thread or a pure silk or cotton. When you find a thread that you and your machine like using it is a reasonably good idea to look first to that particular brand's colour range. Be on the alert, however, for new products to try out and experiment with particularly for embellishment and embroidery purposes.

Without reviewing all the threads on the market by trade names, here are some general guidelines.

For utility stitching (putting things together), seams, zips, most buttonholes etc. etc. use the same thread on the top and in the bobbin underneath.

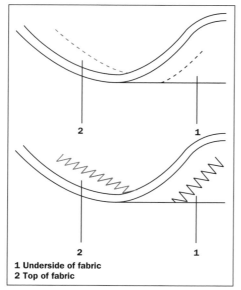

1 Underside of fabric
2 Top of fabric

Pure fabrics/fibres (cotton, silk, wool) can be sewn with 100 per cent cotton '40' or '50'. On silk and wool try 100 per cent silk thread for a pleasant sewing experience and a professional finish. Silk can be very fine like Kinkame or a thicker Gütermann. Pure fabrics can also be sewn with all-purpose thread – but watch the thickness of these threads because they do vary from one manufacturer to another.

Nylons, polyesters and other **synthetics** must be sewn with a synthetic thread and there are many to choose from. It is important to have a certain amount of give or stretch in the thread to match that of the fabric.

Also use these polyester threads on jersey, stretch towelling, plush and knits so that the seams will not pop when you stretch or bend.

Combination fabrics – wool/polyester, polyester/cotton and so on – can be sewn with most threads but if there is more than a small percentage of polyester, favour a polyester or a combination thread.

For decorative stitching there is an amazing choice of threads available. As a complete contrast to utility stitching threads used just for embellishment can break all the rules!

- Compare threads to achieve the effect you are looking for. Doodle some samples and try different stitches with different threads for different effects.

- Fine machine embroidery cotton in a variety of plain and random colours is available and so too are brilliant hues in rayon and other synthetics. There are also fine polyesters, combination threads, medium cottons, pure silks, heavier buttonhole twist and bold threads plus gold and silver so there is an amazing choice.

- Just remember that the modern precision-made sewing machine will not normally take heavy threads on top and in the bobbin because there is not enough room in the raceway: leave a finer thread on the bobbin if you are using a buttonhole twist on the top.

- Match your bobbin thread with the fabric so that you do not need to keep re-threading when you change the top colour.

- Use an ordinary sewing thread in the bobbin and keep the luxury embroidery threads for the top.

- For free embroidery an even greater variety of threads can be used, wound onto the bobbin.

NEEDLE AND THREAD CHART

NEEDLE SIZE	FABRIC TYPE		THREAD TYPE
9-11 (60-70)	**Fine fabrics** Net, organdie, lace, lawn, voile, chiffon, tulle, silk	Natural	Kinkame, Sylko, Sylko Supreme
		Man-made	Molnlyke, Sylko Supreme, Gütermann
11-14 (70-90)	**Lightweight fabrics** Gingham, muslin, fine poplin, taffeta, silk, crêpe-de-chine, seersucker, faille, wool challis	Natural	Kinkame, Sylko, Sylko Supreme
		Man-made and mixtures	Molnlyke, Sylko Supreme, Gütermann
11-14 (70-90)	**Medium weight fabrics** Poplin, cotton, suitings, linen, satin, brocade, velvet, boucle, raw silks, wool crêpe	Natural	Kinkame, Sylko, Sylko Supreme
		Man-made and mixtures	Gütermann Silk, Molnlyke, Sylko Supreme, Gütermann
16-18 (100-110) + Jeans	**Heavyweight fabrics** Tweed, gabardine, flannel, sailcloth, twill, denim, canvas, furnishings	Natural	Sylko, Sylko Supreme, Gütermann Upholstery
		Man-made and mixtures	Sylko Supreme, Gütermann Upholstery
9-11 (60-70) ball or scarfed	**Stretch fabrics** Silk and cotton jersey, polyester jersey, single and double knits, plush, stretch towelling	**Lightweight** Natural	Sylko plus stretch-stitch, otherwise Sylko Supreme (Use stretch stitch wherever possible)
		Lightweight Man-made mixtures	Sylko Supreme or Gütermann
14-18 (90-110) ball or Teflon		**Heavyweight** Natural	Sylko plus stretch-stitch, otherwise Sylko Supreme
		Heavyweight Man-made and mixtures	Sylko Supreme or Gütermann
	SPECIAL FABRICS		
14-16 (90-100)	PVC	Man-made	Sylko Supreme
14-18 (90-110)	Suede/leather and imitation	Natural	Sylko or strong thread
and Leather point		Man-made	Sylko Supreme
11-14 (70-90)	Pure silks and pure medium to heavyweight wools	Natural	Kinkame pure silk Gütermann pure silk
9-14 (60-90) scarfed or ball if appropriate	**TOP STITCHING** **all fabrics . . .**	**Lightweight** **fabrics . . .** all types	Sylko or Sylko Supreme Pure Silk, Embroidery
14-18 (90-110) Teflon if needed		**Medium weight** **fabrics . . .** all types	Sylko, Sylko Supreme, Embroidery: use 2 threads
14-18 (90-110) Teflon if needed		**Heavyweight** fabrics . . . all types	Gütermann button twist, heavy embroidery

NOTE: ALL THE NEEDLES CAN BE USED FOR SPECIAL EFFECTS AND EMBROIDERY PURPOSES

needles and threads

69

trouble shooting

Few sewers are lucky enough to have a sewing room or area where they can leave out their machines and often the sewing machine is brought out hurriedly for a short sewing session.

Haste is the mother and father of many problems! Formulate your own check-list of needles, threads, tensions, stitch selection and so on.

Trouble Shooting

It is truly amazing how many people refuse to consider that they might have inserted the needle wrongly, or mis-threaded through the 'system'!

If everything is done correctly in the first place, you should not get any troubles!

However, usually it is the simple and obvious things that do cause the problems. Even if you have been

But just in case you do . . .

sewing away happily for many, many years you must make allowances for differences between your new and old model.

It is a fact that most complaints with new machines are proven to be this simple error by the user, so you can appreciate why the stores and the manufacturers quiz you when they receive complaints – they are professional people with a desire to help the customer and protect their good name. So, if you have a genuine complaint please do approach the company concerned, but not until you have thoroughly investigated and tested the machine yourself.

- Always thread the machine slowly and carefully – even when you are used to it, because in haste it is so easy to misthread!

- Some problems arise because thread cops or reels spin – particularly when sewing quite fast (e.g. long straight seams) and/or when doing a lot of stopping and starting. Ensure that you have the little red felt cushion on the vertical spindle for your cotton reel to bounce on: it makes for much smoother unravelling.

- On mechanical machines the take-up lever can cause a spin by a jerky start – particularly if it is down when you try to start the machine by de-pressing the foot pedal. Try to cultivate the habit of glancing at the lever and if necessary turn the balance wheel by hand to raise the lever to its highest position before putting your foot down. This will provide a smoother start than placing the needle down in the fabric before you commence.

- The opposite of a spin – complete stop or jerk – also causes problems: in fact the repercussion can be serious because a violent jerk can jam the machine totally and this is a problem that will result in an engineer's call and that can be expensive. This problem usually occurs during fast sewing (again long, straight seams) and with a cotton reel/cop which has a nick cut into the edge to secure the loose end of thread.

During sewing the thread is dashing up and down the reel, the reel is probably 'dancing' a little on the spindle and suddenly the thread and the nick catch together and it does in fact stop the thread moving for a second – quite long enough to do damage. When using this kind of cotton reel make sure that the nick is at the base of the spindle and the problem is most unlikely to occur. The long thin cops do not have a nick but sometimes the top is a little rough and the same problem occurs – have an emery board amongst your sewing kit and do a little smoothing if necessary.

- Always, always turn the balance wheel towards you – never away from you.

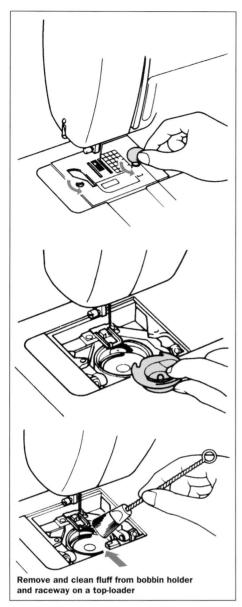

Remove and clean fluff from bobbin holder and raceway on a top-loader

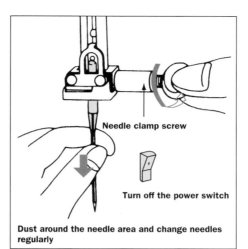

Needle clamp screw

Turn off the power switch

Dust around the needle area and change needles regularly

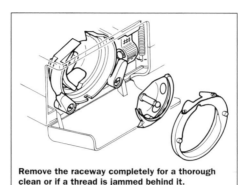

Remove the raceway completely for a thorough clean or if a thread is jammed behind it.

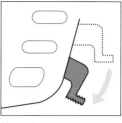

ALWAYS remember to drop the presser foot

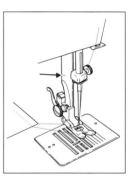

With a mechanical model, hold the threads as you start to sew

ALWAYS pull the fabric and thread out backwards to reduce the strain on the needle

- When you have a machine where you insert the bobbin into a bobbin case and then put both into the raceway you must put the bobbin into the case correctly. In a survey on this one little point it was amazing how many people could not

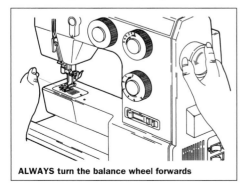

ALWAYS turn the balance wheel forwards

remember how they inserted their bobbins into the case (clockwise or anti-clock wise) and also had no idea that it made any difference to their sewing. It can happen that you will get a spool spin if the bobbin is wrongly inserted so it is worth checking on this.

- It can be infuriating if your thread starts to split and unravel between the needle and the take-up lever. Normally it is not a bad reel of thread but a roughness somewhere on the needle or the machine that the thread is rubbing against. First, change your needle because the eye can be rough. If this does not cure the problem then check all the thread guides very carefully and see if one has a burr – resort to the emery treatment again if you find the roughness. Alternatively, perhaps one of the little wire guides has got slightly squashed and is not allowing the thread through easily. With your tiniest screw driver very carefully enlarge the area that the thread passes through.

- Keep the raceway clean – a build up of fluff can stop the feed dog working altogether. If your machine seems totally dead: check the fuse in the plug before reaching for the phone to call in the repair man: it can save time and money!

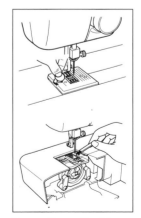

Remove the needle plates and dust out regularly

Sewing Aids

However sophisticated and comprehensive a machine is, it cannot perform total miracles so do not expect them. At the bottom of the range it is even more important to give the machine a helping hand to provide trouble-free and perfect stitches.

■ The most damning thing for any machine is to perform stitches that pucker the fabric.

This is usually caused when a very wide stitch is used on a fine/flimsy fabric and the pull of the thread causes the puckering. To overcome the problem, make the stitch width narrower OR support the fabric during stitching. Support can be obtained in two ways:

Interfacings will support the stitches so use one of suitable weight for the job in hand. In dressmaking the normal rules apply but in crafts and creative stitching, for instance, heavy pelmet weight Vilene (or similar) can be used for bulk as well as support for the stitches. Experiment with various fabrics, stitches and interfacings and observe the results for future use. Interfacings are the ideal support for stitching where the back of the project will remain unseen in use of display.

Stitch and Tear was developed to support stitches during sewing but to be easily torn away on completion of the design. This product (also from Vilene) is normally used when the reverse of the project will be on view during use, for instance table linen and sheer fabrics. Stitch and Tear is also widely used behind the fabric inside a hoop for motif and embroidery unit work. It can also be used behind fabrics during faggotting to hold the fabrics in place as well as supporting the stitches.

A particular benefit of S and T over using paper, is that tiny pieces trapped behind stitches will pass through the laundry/dry cleaning process without problems.

Water soluble fabric resembles a layer of plastic and it can be successfully used to support stitches on a fine fabric but it can also be used alone for special effects. By stitching directly onto the water soluble medium a form of lace can be stitched/manufactured which can be used in a variety of creative ways for embellishments.

Bondaweb

■ Very uneven stitching can be caused when fabrics move or 'ride' on each other as they pass through the machine and this can be particularly infuriating with appliqué work . . .

Bondaweb overcomes this by fusing the two (or more!) layers together BEFORE stitching, thus holding them in the exact position required. Bondaweb is a layer of grease-proof-type paper with a layer of adhesive spread over one side: it can be cut to size/shape before use, or a sheet applied to a piece of fabric which is cut to shape afterwards. Because it is opaque, designs can be traced onto it. Items fused by Bondaweb can also be laundered or dry cleaned safely.

Wadding/batting will emphasise decorative stitching as well as supporting the stitches and prove the ideal backing substance.

■ Throwing the stitches into 'relief' and adding a third dimension to the stitch-craft can be attractive as well as a 'trick' to provide perfect stitches!

■ If a backing medium of any kind is out of the question for the project in hand a HOOP can be used to stretch and support the fabric during stitching. Many find a hoop restrictive on a large design or piece of work whilst others have never considered abandoning the hoop in favour of some of the sewing aids mentioned above.

Machines with an embroidery unit utilise the hoop to construct the design and so it cannot be abandoned and in most cases the addition of the backing fabric is used AS WELL.

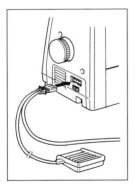

Remember to unplug your machine when you have finished stitching . . .

. . . and cover the machine to keep it free from dust!

CHECK LIST

Trouble Free Sewing

■ DO have your machine on a firm and stable table, at a comfortable height.

■ DO have a comfortable and stable chair.

■ DO have adequate lighting.

■ DO keep your machine spotlessly clean and free from dust and fluff.

■ DO make sure the needle is inserted the right way round!

■ DO thread the machine slowly and carefully.

■ DO always pull the work out of the machine backwards.

■ DO hold onto the threads as you begin to sew with a mechanical machine.

■ DO enjoy playing with the machine and experimenting.

■ DO NOT twiddle the tension knob indiscriminately!

■ DO NOT tackle a BIG new venture on a brand new machine before experimenting with your new range of stitches and techniques.

glossary

Appliqué
A design cut out from one fabric and applied by stitches to another fabric.

Asymmetric
An uneven or out-of-proportion design.

Attachments
General term for extra machine pieces, i.e. presser foot, quilting guide.

Automatic de-clutch
Modern machines have an automatic clutch which disconnects when the bobbin winding mechanism is engaged. On older machines (and some of the basic or modestly-priced modern machines) the clutch is disconnected manually by the twisting of a plate/disc inside the balance wheel.

Automatic lock-off
On some computer models the machine will sew several locking stitches on the spot and the machine will then stop sewing in the needle-up position. The threads can then be snipped off close to the stitches.

Automatic machine
Most modern mechanical machines are 'automatic' – all the stitches (utility or embroidery) are produced by the machine with the aid of cams. When the particular stitch or design is selected the cam ensures the needle-swing movement is correctly altered during the sewing sequence.

Automatic tension
Now a common feature on very many models, the tension self adjusts for fabric and thread being used. For the majority of stitching it is an excellent system. The tension can be manually adjusted, or over-ridden on a computer, for any fine tuning required on unusual projects.

Balance wheel
Situated on the far right of the machine head, the wheel varies in size according to the model and make of machine. By manually turning the wheel the needle can be raised and lowered. The balance wheel should always be turned forwards – never backwards – when the machine is threaded, otherwise extra loops of thread could cause the machine to jam.

Ballpoint needle
Developed for sewing the modern synthetic fabrics and jerseys, these needles have a slightly rounded point which will slide to one side or the other of the fibres in the fabric. Ballpoint needles will also eliminate some of the 'skipped-stitch' problems common with this type of fabric. See also Scarfed needle.

Bar tack
The end stitches which are the full width of the buttonhole are termed bar tacks: they can also be used to reinforce the end of an opening or seam detail. Many computer machines now have a special selection for this other purpose.

Basting
Originally an American term for 'tacking', now universally used for machine tacking.

Batting
Wadding used in quilting and other padded items – American term.

Bias
A true diagonal of 45° across the warp and weft of the fabric.

Blind hem
Type of hem where most of the stitches are on the 'turned-up' piece of fabric and only an occasional stitch is on the body of the garment. Dextrous handling can minimise the visibility of the stitch on the right side but it should be stressed that this is not an 'invisible' method of hemming.

Blind hem foot
Special presser foot to assist with blind hemming.

Blind hem guide
Small metal guide inserted between the presser foot and the presser foot screw to assist with blind hemming. The blind hem foot has virtually taken over from the guide.

Bobbin
Small circular spool in plastic or metal inserted into the machine to hold the underneath thread.

Bobbin case
Small, metal, cylindrical case into which some bobbins are placed before insertion into the

machine. There is an adjustable tension spring incorporated.

Bobbin holder
On top loading machines this will hold a bobbin during stitching: it also incorporates an adjustable tension spring.

Braid
Narrow trimming of various kinds used to embellish garments.

Button sewing
It is unlikely that the sewing machine would be taken out just to sew on a button! However, when completing a garment it is useful to sew on buttons in this way because unlike ready-to-wear garments the buttons are sewn with a lock stitch. Any zig-zag machine will sew on a button merely by dropping the feed dog and some machines will have a special foot supplied. On some models an alternative needle plate is fitted when it is not possible to lower the feed dog.

Buttonhole
A slit in a garment through which to pass a button. Various types can be produced automatically on modern machines and on top models the choice may be as large as 7 or more. The normal straight-ended buttonhole can be produced on any basic zig-zag machine.

Buttonhole twist
Heavy thread ideal for sewing on buttons but not for sewing machine buttonholes because the thread is too heavy and thick for this purpose. It is, however, a very useful thread for top stitching and embroidery work.

Cam
Disc of metal, strengthened plastic or nylon with a shaped edge for variable motion of the needle. Present in a mechanical machine to control automatic stitching.

Cassettes
Interchangeable cassettes, popular on some computer machines as a means of programming.

Chain looper
A circular piece resembling a bobbin case to insert into the machine instead of the bobbin and/or bobbin case whilst sewing a chain stitch. Although once popular, they are now a rarity.

Chain stitch
A line of stitching with one continuous thread which resembles a series of links. By its nature it will unravel when one end is pulled, making it useful as a tacking stitch. However, it can of course be fastened off and used for various decorative purposes.

Clip-on feet
A general term for presser feet which can clip or pull on/off of an ankle piece screwed to the machine in the usual way. This feature is now widely used and makes changing feet quick and easy.

Colour coding
To assist with setting controls on semi-automatic, automatic and some basic computer machines the selector dials/knobs often have a system of colour coding. Thus the symbol of the pattern on the stitch selector will tie in with the same colour on the stitch-width control and the stitch-length control too. This helps the operator to ensure that stitches are easily set to the required standard.

Computer machine
Working with 'chip' technology and step motors computers use less moving parts than mechanical models. Because of the vast memory capabilities, these machines can hold millions of stitch permutations and utilise excellent control facilities for using the machine.

Concealed (invisible) zip
A specialist item easily inserted into garments but it is invisible in use – when closed the zipper resembles a normal seam line. An extremely proficient method of closure particularly on problem fabrics it is ideal for all weights of fabrics and all types of garment. Use an invisible zipper foot for simple insertion.

Cord
A fine rope or string which can be plain or decorative. Encased by bias fabric and inserted into a seam line it will provide a decorative/contrasting feature: a decorative cord can be applied or couched on top of the fabric for embellishment.

Cording
In sewing machine terms cording means to couch the cords in a decorative way on to the fabric – one or more cords can be used.

Correcting
On computer machines the facility to review the sequence programmed by the user and to make corrections as necessary: this usually means cancelling out the program sequence after the mistaken letter or pattern.

Couching
A term used for a technique whereby a cord or thread of any thickness is laid on to the fabric and held there by a finer thread being sewn in a decorative manner over it. On a modern machine various stitches are suitable for this medium.

Craft stitches
A range of stitches incorporated into a machine which falls between basic utility stitches and complicated embroidery. They

glossary

may have a particular use for functional techniques or be quite decorative.

Cross stitch
Thought to be the oldest embroidery stitch in the world and now available on computer machines.

Darn
To repair a worn or torn fabric by various stitches. Tricot stitch is one of the best automatic stitches for this purpose, but others are suitable. Automatic-darn sequences are contained on some computer machines.

Darning foot
Free darning can be done in a similar way to free embroidery by moving the fabric around under the special darning foot. As the needle goes up and down the hook over the needle clamp causes the foot to rise and fall with the needle: thus the fabric is held tautly whilst the needle passes through the fabric but it is possible to move the fabric freely whilst the needle is out. This foot can also be used to do expert monograms and free embroidery. Often called a 'hopper foot'.

De-clutch bobbin winding
A modern system of bobbin winding whereby the bobbin on its winding peg is pushed into a locked position and the clutch is automatically freed. This ensures that the needle does not rise and fall during winding. Older models and more basic new machines require manual release of the clutch by turning the inside disc on the balance wheel.

Decorative stitches
A range of stitches automatically selected to provide embellishment rather than utilitarian use.

Digital display readout
On some computer machines an LCD 'window' displaying in numerical terms the stitch selection chosen by the operator.

Doodle cloth
Firm cotton cloth for practice stitching.

Double lift
By raising the presser foot lever higher than the usual raised position the foot 'double lifts' to allow thick fabrics to be placed beneath it.

Double-edged zig-zag
A superb over-casting stitch on some computer machines.

Dual feed
Exclusive to Pfaff the dual feed is a lever which pulls down between the prongs of the presser foot and so gives extra control over feeding the fabric. Other makes of machines utilise the Walking/Even Feed Foot to do the same job.

Easy thread
Most manufacturers now incorporate the easy threading system on the majority of their machines. The system ensures that the thread slots into position through take-up lever, thread guides etc. and does not need to be threaded through any holes until it reaches the needle eye.

Editing
On computer machines, the facility to review the sequence programmed into the machine by the user, and to make alterations without cancelling out all the sequence in so doing.

Electronic machine
Not to be confused with computers, electronic machines are mechanical with electronic features. These are usually in the foot pedal exercising greater control over the machine and can also be used for stitch selection by using LED. Needle control can be electronic and LCD screens are another feature: these can show stitch information and sometimes HELP! data to assist the user.

Electronic needle control
This usually means that the needle is electronically controlled to always complete the sewing/stitch cycle and thus stop with the needle in the up position.

Elongated stitch length
Some computer machines can be programmed to elongate a design without destroying the shape or the stitch density.

Extension plate/table
Either a removable or additional sewing area around the needle plate and/or free arm. Most dressmakers successfully use the free arm working area for all their work but when tackling larger articles a bigger sewing area can be helpful. Extension plates can clip on, slide in, pull up, pull down, fold away, be built in or supplied separately!

Eyelet
This facility is now popular on computer machines and some models will have a variety of sizes available. A mechanical machine will need an eyelet plate to do the work successfully.

Faggotting
A technique where two pieces of fabric are held together with a decorative stitch, such as a feather stitch, to provide an open-work seam.

Feather stitch
A hand-embroidery stitch which has transferred well to the sewing machine, with many decorative uses. Traditionally used for faggotting and for crazy patchwork. Because it incorporates a back-stitch it is also very elastic and

can be used as a utility stitch on stretch fabrics.

Feed dog
A small plate of parallel metal teeth which feeds the fabric through the machine and under the needle. It is altering the movement of the feed dog which does, in fact, alter the stitch length.

Felt disc
A little (usually red) felt 'cushion' which is placed over the thread spindle for the cotton reel to sit on to give smooth unravelling of the thread and eliminate, where possible, reel spin during sewing.

Flat bed machine
Traditionally shaped machine with a flat base plate.

Foot control
The foot control/pedal will vary in size and shape dramatically from model to model but all have the same function: to control the speed of the stitching.

Free arm machine
Machine with an 'arm' with adequate space around it to enable sleeves, trouser legs, armholes and other difficult items to be positioned more easily under the needle. Most machines now have this facility including quite modest and low priced ones.

Free machine embroidery
This is an art form in its own right and NOT the built-in or pre-programmed embroidery stitches available by turning a dial, knob or lever on your machine. Free embroidery can be done on any machine at all – even a straight-stitch model or top computer – and it is necessary only to drop the feed dog and remove the presser foot completely or alternatively use a hopper foot. Some machines provide a special needle plate that fixes over the normal one instead of dropping the feed dog but these are in the minority. The fabric should be supported by an embroidery hoop or backing medium and then moved freely beneath the needle. The presser foot lever MUST be put down during sewing or there is no tension on the thread.

Gathering
A process to reduce or control the fullness of a fabric by passing two lines of stitching through the fabric at maximum stitch length and then pulling up the BOBBIN (underneath) threads, both rows together, to reduce the fabric to the required length. Gathers should be evenly distributed along the length and this is best achieved by 'stroking' the gathers with a pin. Gathers can be very full for decoration or for easing a large piece into a small space such as a sleeve heading.

Zig-zag gathering
is an alternative to shirring it is a soft and supple gathering for blouses, lingerie and children's clothes. Hold the cord elastic firmly in front and behind the presser foot and stretch the elastic – not the fabric. Sew a row of zig-zag stitches OVER the elastic, being careful not to catch the elastic with the needle. A shirring elastic can be used, or a fine cord/hat elastic and pulled up and knotted when sewing is completed.

Hand control
A method of stopping and starting the machine by hand rather than the foot pedal: it can be a push button on the machine or a separate control held in the hand.

Help!
Many computers have read-out facilities to cope with problems which is activated by the menu within. Electronic models may have a similar, but less comprehensive, method of displaying messages.

Hopping foot
A darning or embroidery foot with a spring or lever to enable it to hop up and down as the needle rises and falls.

Interfacing
In dressmaking this is a medium placed between the outside fabric and facing to hold, mould, shape and/or support both stitches and the main fabric. It is most important to use interfacing and to be guided by the pattern instructions.
Interfacing can also be used to support stitchery on a fine fabric, i.e. embroidered motifs, buttonholes.
Interfacing is available in woven and non-woven mediums and is a very necessary aid and support to modern sewing. 'Vilene' has become something of a generic term for non-woven interfacing.

Invisible zipper (see concealed zip)

Knee lift
A right-angled metal 'rod' which inserts into the machine to enable the presser foot to be raised or lowered by touching it with the knee. Only used by Bernina machines at the time of going to press.

Lateral stitching
Various top of the range computers can stitch in any direction without turning the fabric under the needle.

LCD
Initial letters for 'Liquid Crystal Display.' This is the system used for read-out panels on computer and electronic machines.

LED
Initial letters for 'Light Emitting Diode.' On

electronic and computer machines the small (usually red) light beside the selected pattern; or sometimes used as a warning light, i.e. bobbin running out.

Lock stitch
All machines that use a top and bottom thread produce a lock stitch, i.e. the threads meet, twist and lock together with every stitch made.

Lock-a-matic
On computer machines a sequence where the machine is programmed to automatically sew a few reverse stitches at the beginning of the seam before forward sewing commences: on some it will also do the reverse stitches automatically again at the end of the seam.

Lurex
A metallic, untarnished thread, which can be woven or knitted into fabrics.

Machine embroidery
Patterns/designs sewn automatically by the machine produced by means of cams or programmed by computer.

Manufacturer's handbook/manual
The instruction booklet that comes with the new sewing machine.

Mechanical Machine
A machine which works with cogs and cams rather than a computer system.

Memory
Computer machines have pre-programmed stitch sequences and other controls held in 'memory' i.e. on the computer chip. Similarly, this term is used for a memory bank for the user to recall his/her own stitch sequences.

Memory card/smart card
Tucking inside the computer machine or scanner, the card will act as an extra memory bank for the individual creative designs and stitch sequences. Many manufacturers supply pre-programmed cards to extend the range of stitches and designs available.

Mercerised cotton
Named after John Mercer who discovered the process to give cotton thread a silk-like sheen (in 1844). Sylko is the most famous but other companies use this process too.

Mirror image
Computer machines have the facility to 'turn over' a pattern to provide a mirror image of themselves. Patterns may be turned from side-to-side or end-to-end depending on the capability of each model.

Monograms
This is the term for a large letter(s) used to embellish and personalise a particular garment or craft item. Many machines will do small sized letters – up to 9mm depending on the model. Some will do larger letters by lateral stitching and others even bigger by using an embroidery unit.

Motif
In sewing machine terminology, this is a complete design which the machine will perform and lock off. It may be in a number of colours using an embroidery unit, or a single colour with or without a unit.

Needle
Long, thin, steel instrument with a point and eye at one end which when threaded passes through the fabric to create the stitches. Various types are available.

Needle clamp
Holds the needle in position in the machine.

Needle plate
Plate that surrounds the feed dog: often graduated as a guide to show various widths of seam allowance. Some elderly models need the plate exchanged for straight-stitch or zig-zag sewing. Machines that do not have the facility to drop the feed dog usually have a specialist needle-plate or needle-plate cover to allow for free movement of fabric for darning or free embroidery.

Needle penetration
The force with which the needle goes through the fabric is the penetration: electronic and computer machines will have greater controlled penetration than a normal mechanical machine allowing it to stitch through thick or multi-layered fabrics with exceptional ease.

Needle positions
Refers to the position of the needle within the width of the presser foot during straight sewing. Some machines have one position only whilst some have left, middle and right needle positions. Electronic and computer machines can have anything from 'one' to 'unlimited' needle positions but a comprehensive top model could be expected to have approximately twelve. This facility is extremely useful because it ensures that the fabric is held firmly and securely under the foot whilst the needle can be moved to sew exactly where the stitching is required: e.g. on the very edge of the fabric, at a specifically graduated distance for top stitching, setting the width of the seam to ¼" for patchwork.

Needle swing
The movement of the needle from side to side within the width of the presser foot.

Needle threader
A variety of types are available. They are

usually set above and to the left of the needle and are pulled down into position whilst in use and then stowed away again when sewing is in progress.

Needle up/down control

Normally a small button on the facia on electronic or computer machines which is depressed to lower the needle into the fabric when required, i.e. turning a corner. Others require a tap on the foot pedal. This alleviates turning the balance wheel as on less sophisticated machines.

By this method some models can always stop with needle down OR needle up depending on the work in hand.

Outline zig-zag

A stretch stitch for bulked fabrics which gives a Z-shaped effect because two small stitches are sewn side by side and then the fabric is pushed forwards and the machine stitches two more small stitches side by side. It is a very narrow stitch. When the seam is opened out this small degree of width is lost in the bulk of the fabric. A useful, firm and stretchy stitch for this type of fabric which gives excellent results.

Overlock

The use of two or more threads to encase a raw edge. Three threads provide a seam and seam neatening and overlockers with four or more threads are also available. It is usual to have the two seam allowances overlocked together to provide a narrow neatened seam 9-12mm (⅜"-½") wide and the overlock machine will trim off the surplus fabric to this width.

A normal domestic sewing machine will not overlock but does similar 'over-edge' finishing. Only an Overlocker will do a true overlock stitch.

Over-ride/manual adjuster

On computer machines this allows the operator to over-ride the programmed settings of the machine and make his or her own fine adjustments or alterations to the stitches or stitch sequences.

Oversewing/overcasting

Neatening a raw edge with a zig-zag, tricot stitch or other specialist stitch on the machine.

Patch-o-matic

(see pressure regulator)

Pattern

An embroidery or fancy stitch is often referred to as a 'pattern' rather than a 'stitch'.

Pictogram

A method of building up designs by using pre-formed blocks of satin stitches and unique to Viking/Husqvarna at the time of going to press.

Pin

A fine wire with a point at one end and a knob at the other, modern pins are usually made of stainless steel. Available in various lengths for different purposes. Glass-headed pins are extremely useful for dressmaking and craft work and are long enough to sew over (at right angles to the stitching line).

Pin tuck

A machine pin tuck is sewn with the twin needle. The bobbin-thread tension is tightened so that in sewing the two top threads pull together, thus creating a neat little tuck. This is very effective on a soft jersey fabric when rows and rows of tucks are the focal design feature.

Piping

A fine cord enclosed in a bias-cut tube of fabric which is inserted for decorative purposes into a seam. Can be used in dressmaking, upholstery work or craft work.

It is possible to purchase insertion-piping by the metre – this is a fine cord which is woven on a 'self strip' of fabric: the strip is sewn into the seam allowing the cord to be exposed.

Plug

It is important to have the correct wiring and fuse in the electric plug attached to the mains electricity supply.

When leaving the sewing machine unattended, the mains switch of the machine should be switched off or the plug removed from the socket-outlet.

When servicing the sewing machine or when removing covers or changing lamps, the machine must be disconnected from the supply by removing the plug from the socket-outlet.

Plush

Plush is a fabric with a longer nap than that of velvet. Originally made with pure fibres (cotton, wool, silk) but now widely available as a stretch fabric in polyester and used extensively for leisure wear.

Presser foot

The small foot that is fixed to the machine around the needle, which together with the feed dog holds the fabric whilst the machine is sewing: a variety of presser feet is provided with machines for producing various stitching techniques.

Presser foot lever

The lever by which you raise and lower the presser foot. Many modern machines have this lever to the right of the needle under the arch of the head of the machine so that it is easily moved with the right hand rather than at the back: it is indeed very practical when you get used to this different position. On most machines the lever can be raised to a second, higher, position to enable very thick fabric to be easily inserted under the foot.

glossary

Presser foot screw

On basic machines the screw holds the presser foot on to the machine. On very many models there is a unit (ankle) onto which the presser foot can be clipped or snapped. This is a fast-exchange method for normal sewing; however, more intricate feet such as rufflers, still need to be fixed by the presser foot screw in the accepted manner and in these instances the clip-on foot ankle unit needs to be removed.

Pressure regulator

An adjustable unit to determine the amount of pressure placed on to the feed dog by the presser foot. The pressure is extremely important in holding the fabric so that the feed dog can determine the stitch length accurately. Insufficient pressure may result in poor feeding, skipped stitches and difficulty in guiding the fabric. Too much pressure can damage the fabric. On many machines the dial to regulate the pressure is inside the face plate cover over the needle/light area; on older and basic machines it is usually an adjustable silver bolt-type regulator on top of the machine which is adjusted by screwing it up or down. Another spring loaded adjuster is called Patch-o-matic.

Programme

On a computer machine, a stitch sequence put into memory by the machine operator or pre-programmed by the manufacturer.

Programming

On computer machines, putting the programme into memory by the machine user.

Quick-darn

An automatic, pre-programmed darning sequence in some computer machines.

Quilting

A technique to stitch together at least two, usually three layers of fabric to give a padded effect. Originally developed to provide warm, protective clothing, it can also be used purely decoratively.

Quilting guide

A curved metal bar which is attached to the sewing machine and serves as a guide to the consecutive rows of stitches in the quilting process. Quilting guides attach to machines in various ways but all are extremely simple.

Reverse feed

Backwards sewing

Ric-rac stitch

A zig-zag triple stitch used on stretch fabrics in any area where a zig-zag would normally be used because it is a stretch zig-zag. It can also be used effectively for top stitching.

Roller foot

A presser foot with small, scored rollers which will both grip and glide over problem fabrics such as PVC, leather, velvets and plush.

Ruffling

Frills are usually gathered along one side to provide the fullness, in ruffling the fullness is a series of tiny pleats.

Ruffler

A large presser foot which pushes the fabric to be ruffled into pleats of exact size: the size of the pleat can be altered by a simple adjustment to the foot.

Saddle stitch

Originally in hand sewing this was a running stitch in a heavy thread to give a decorative finish to the edge of coats and other tailored garments. On the machine a very long straight stitch is usually used to try to copy this effect but the latest machines have developed various sequences of stitching (often incorporating reverse stitches) to provide a decorative saddle stitch.

Satin stitch

A zig-zag of any width but where the stitch length has been adjusted to allow the threads to lay closely together, side by side.

Scallop

Derived from the shape of the shellfish, a scalloped edge is one of continuous semi-circles. On some machines there are various stitch sequences to give a scalloped edge of various styles using satin stitching, open stitching or even straight-stitch sewing which can be adjusted to give large or very tiny scallops.

Scanner

A scanner can be used alongside some computer machines to transfer a drawn/printed design onto a Memory/smart card. When the card is placed into the machine, the design which was scanned is stitched onto the fabric.

Scarfed needle

An improved type of ballpoint needle where the cut-away piece above the needle eye has been extended in length. This needle was developed for jersey and polyester fabrics but will sew all light-to medium weight fabrics very successfully including silk, cotton and light weight wool.

Seam guide

(a) Guide lines scored or printed on to the needle plate.

(b) An adjustable attachment which fits beside the needle plate to determine the width of the seam allowance.

Shell edging

Usually used for lingerie or in baby wear. A narrow, turned hem is sewn with the blind

GLOSSARY

hem stitch to draw the hem into a small shell-like shape.

Shell tuck
Used in lingerie, baby wear and blouses it provides a dainty alternative to a straight tuck. It is sewn in the same manner as the shell edging.

Shirring
Shirring in modern terms refers to rows of gathering with an elastic thread although it originally was a term to describe a piece gathered with rows and rows of stitches to give a ruffled effect. The elastic thread is wound on to the bobbin, rows of stitches are sewn and finally drawn up to the required size.

With the enormous scope of the modern sewing machine stitches and the latest developments in haberdashery there are now many acceptable (and easier!) alternatives to shirring that produce the same effect and are stronger in wear.

Shuttle hook
Mechanism into which the bobbin case fits.

Side cutter
A large, specialist presser foot containing a knife which trims excessive fabric from the seam allowance whilst overcasting.

Sleeve arm
see free arm machine.

Slide plate
Sliding top cover to drop-in bobbin area.

Smocking
A decorative effect where evenly spaced rows of gathers are drawn up to the required size and held in place with ornamental stitches. Machine smocking is not as regular as hand smocking but is most effective and very many of the machine embroidery stitches are suitable.

Speed control
Some models contain two speed settings for speed control: fast and slow. This can be on the head of the machine or on the foot pedal. It is advisable to use the machine normally on fast and get good control by use of the foot pedal as this is less likely to burn out the motor than constant heavy use whilst set at slow. On computer machines one-stitch-at-a-time control is possible using the foot pedal on a fast setting.

Spool holder
Cotton-reel holder on top of the machine to hold the top thread – this can be horizontal inside or horizontal/vertical outside the machine casing.

Stitches
Each time the needle passes through the fabric and the bobbin completes it's circuit to link the two threads a stitch is formed. In general terms, each different pattern is usually called a stitch.

Stitch indicator
Panel of diagrammed stitches on the machine facia beside which a movable needle/light (LED) or similar, indicates which automatic stitch has been selected and/or programmed. On a computer machine the stitch indicator could be a moving read-out in digital numbers or the picture of the stitch on the LCD screen.

Stitch length control
On a mechanical machine this is the lever, knob or dial to manually adjust the length of the stitch. Touch button or touch screen control is used on many computer models.

Stitch modifier
A fine-tuner adjustment for altering stitch density on buttonholes, etc.

Stitch selector
A dial, lever, push button or sensor screen on the machine facia which is used to select required automatic and pre-programmed stitches.

Stitch-width control
Similar to stitch length (above) and used to adjust the swing of the needle (i.e. the zig-zag width).

Stop/start button
Used to stop and start the machine when a foot pedal is not required.

Take-up lever
Lever above the needle through which the thread passes and which goes up and down during sewing, pulling the thread required for the stitching process off the top reel of thread.

Technique
A term for a purpose to which a stitch is put and often requiring a specialist presser foot.

Teflon needle
A needle coated with Teflon or similar carbon-type substance which was developed for smoothly stitching synthetic fabrics, particularly jersey and waddings.

Tension
The tightness of the threads when making stitches is termed 'tension'. Traditionally, there is a dial to alter the top thread tension via the 'tension unit' and an adjustable screw to alter the tension of the bobbin on the bobbin case. Many models now have automatic tension, but it can still be altered for fine tuning. Drop-in, top loading bobbins will still

have a screw incorporated for adjustment. Even without automatic tension, the top tension should rarely require altering except when specialist threads or techniques are being used.

Tension discs
Twin discs within the tension unit through which the thread MUST pass for the tension to be effective. Can be inside or outside the machine casing.

Thread (1)
All embracing term to cover a spun-out filament of yarn of cotton, silk, polyester, poly/cotton etc. etc.

Thread (2)
Passing through the thread (1) through the correct system – including tension unit – on the machine.

Thread cutter
Small sharp cutter to snick sewing threads. Older machines and some basic models have a sharp area in the back of the presser foot bar, but the latest machines are incorporating extremely sharp and efficient cutters adjacent to the sewing area. Some models also provide another cutter beside the bobbin winder.

Top stitch
In dressmaking a top stitch is a line of stitching to emphasise a seam line, the edge of collar, cuffs, lapel or hemline. It can be a row of very long straight stitches, a special saddle stitch or similar or decorative stitches if suitable. Top stitching is also a simple adornment in craft work and upholstery.

Touch sensitive screen
LCD screens on many top of the computer machines are touch sensitive for selecting stitches and general control of the machine.

Tricot stitch (three-stitch zig-zag)
A zig-zag-shaped stitch with three stitches on each zig and zag! An effective stretch stitch and better than basic zig-zag for overcasting /neatening.

Triple needle
A three-pronged needle for decorative work.

Triple stretch stitch
The true straight stretch stitch. It incorporates a reverse stitch every third stitch and is an effective straight seam line for heavier stretch fabrics. Extremely strong it can also be used on non-stretch fabrics when a heavy or very secure seam is required. Also effective as a decorative top stitch when a saddle stitch is not available.

Twin needle
A two-pronged needle for decorative work.

Underbed trimmer
By pressing a button on the machine the sewing threads are snipped thus eliminating the use of scissors or a traditional thread cutter on the machine. Only on some Brother machines at the time of going to press.

Utility stitch (working stitch)
A stitch used primarily for construction techniques, i.e. zig-zag, overcast, hemming, stretch stitch.

Velvet
A dense, short-piled fabric of cotton or man-made fibres. The pile can cause problems when it is sewn by machine because it tends to 'walk'. Use a specialist foot such as a Walking/even-feed foot.

Wing needle
Needle that has two wings each side of the eye to enlarge the hole in the fabric during sewing. It is also possible to obtain a twin-wing needle. The decorative effect is particularly used in Heirloom sewing.

Working stitch
see utility stitch.

Zig-zag
A line of stitching where the needle swings from side to side taking a stitch each time.

Zig-zag machine
A term used for a basic machine which will only sew straight stitch and zig-zag.

Zig-zag gathering
see gathering.

Zipper foot
A specialist foot for zipper insertion. There are a variety of different styles available but all work well. They can also be used to insert piping. Invisible zippers need to be inserted with an invisible-zipper foot, not an ordinary zipper foot.

index

notes

notes